The New Fibonacci
Trader Workbook

WILEY TRADING

The New Fibonacci Trader Workbook

Step-by-Step Exercises to Help You Master The New Fibonacci Trader

ROBERT FISCHER

JOHN WILEY & SONS

This publication is designed to provide accurate and authoritative information in regard to the subject matter covered. It is sold with the understanding that the publisher is not engaged in rendering professional services. If professional advice or other expert assistance is required, the services of a competent professional person should be sought.

ISBN 0-471-09217-7

Printed in the United States of America.

10 9 8 7 6 5 4 3 2 1

ACKNOWLEDGMENTS

In March 2001, Pamela van Giessen, managing editor at John Wiley & Sons, New York, asked me if I was interested in writing a workbook to complement *The New Fibonacci Trader*. I accepted enthusiastically because I knew it would give me a chance to present the Fibonacci trading tools in a different format.

Readers of *The New Fibonacci Trader* can enhance and test their knowledge through the questions/answers and exercises in this easy-to-read workbook. Readers who are starting with the workbook can later move on to *The New Fibonacci Trader* and the accompanying WINPHI software, which will enable them to work, in real time, with PHI-ellipses, PHI-spirals, and PHI-channels.

The most difficult challenge, when writing this workbook, was the transition from the academic language of *The New Fibonacci Trader* to a straightforward and hands-on approach. Laurie A. Frederik was of tremendous help in accomplishing this task. Her expertise in converting complex analytic trading concepts into easy-to-understand questions and answers created the necessary bridge to readers.

My main objective here is to help traders utilize the geometrical Fibonacci trading tools successfully. Traders have their own terminology and special ways of expressing themselves. Anne Cavanagh, of Green Valley, Arizona, added these viewpoints through her in-depth knowledge of the Fibonacci trading concept.

Fibonacci trading tools are best understood visually, through defined charts. My son, Dr. Jens Fischer, who worked very closely with me to write *The New Fibonacci Trader,* was of extraordinary help in producing the charts and the page layout of the workbook.

Writing this workbook was an enjoyable challenge. I thank all the people who gave me the opportunity to share my ideas and my experience.

R. F.

The following figures in this book are related to this disclaimer: 2.8, 2.9, 3.22, 3.25, 3.26, 3.27, 3.30, 3.31, 3.32, 5.22, 5.23, 5.24, 8.2, 8.3.

WHY THIS WORKBOOK?

This workbook directly follows the structure of *The New Fibonacci Trader*. Each chapter includes a summary of the key terms and concepts. After each summary, the knowledge of the reader is tested with **questions** and **exercises.**

Utilizing this workbook will benefit those who have already read the textbook, for they can easily refer to the shortened summaries of complex concepts, and deepen their mastery of concept application with exercises.

The novice, on the other hand, will receive an introduction to the rationale behind Fibonacci trading strategies, and may then proceed to the textbook and begin real-time applications with the WINPHI software package.

The Fibonacci tools presented, and their application strategies, are complex, and traders must first gain an in-depth understanding of the foundational concepts. The workbook format includes summaries of the most important rules, and examples that introduce the Fibonacci trading tools. The questions and exercises then provide excellent testing and clarification of one's understanding.

Because this workbook is intended to be an introduction and/or a supplement, it does not include the CD-ROM with the WINPHI software, which is packaged with each copy of the textbook. Readers who wish to work with the historical data and graphics necessary for analysis and practical application will find the software package particularly rewarding.

The workbook gives beginners an opportunity to decide whether they wish to adopt the Fibonacci concept and trading strategy. Obviously, it is easier to work with simple crossover moving averages than with PHI-spirals or PHI-ellipses. Traders must decide whether they want to work with conventional technical trading tools—which, by design, lag behind the market action—or to learn the more complex trading tools that are able to anticipate precalculated turning points in the markets, and therefore allow early investing and higher profits.

Gaining an understanding of the fundamental Fibonacci summation series and the ratios derived by this sequence is not easy. There are many ways to apply the trading tools, and success depends on the skill, experience, and risk preference of the trader. The particular time compression used also greatly affects the analysis and trading technique. Although the way the trading tools are applied does not change, working with 15-minute data requires greater discipline than working with weekly data.

One of the biggest drawbacks of describing trading strategies in a book is that, after publication, there is no way to update charts or strategies with new data. We are in a dynamic marketplace, and strategies that work today may not work in the future. However, we strongly believe that the Fibonacci trading devices described here, and in the textbook, will remain effective, regardless of the marketplace and the product analyzed, as long as volatility and marketability are present.

This trading concept is available on the Internet at **www.fibotrader.com,** where we will continuously update data and upgrade software.

All examples and strategies in this workbook have been developed to the very best of my knowledge. I do not offer fully automated trading approaches, but readers are introduced to some previously unknown possibilities of beating the markets.

This workbook is intended to be educational. All the concepts are presented with detailed examples. I hope that readers find my ideas inspiring, enlightening, and useful, and can share in my excitement regarding their possibilities.

Zug, Switzerland   ROBERT FISCHER
August 2001

CONTENTS

1

BASIC FIBONACCI PRINCIPLES

Let your imagination soar. This phrase is the overarching introduction to the fascination of the findings of *Leonardo Di Pisa,* commonly known as *Fibonacci,* and a long-lasting appeal to creativity and imagination.

The first chapter on basic Fibonacci principles is subdivided into five major parts: (1) Leonardo Fibonacci; (2) the Fibonacci summation series; (3) the Fibonacci ratio in nature and geometry; (4) the Elliott wave principle; and (5) geometrical Fibonacci trading tools.

LEONARDO FIBONACCI

Although the name Fibonacci has become more and more popular in the analysis of stocks, stock index futures, cash currencies, and commodities, little is known about the person himself.

Leonardo Fibonacci (filius Bonacci), alias Leonardo of Pisa (1170–1240), lived and worked as a merchant and mathematician in Pisa, Italy. His early years were spent in a Christian community, but he received his education among Mohammedans of Barbary. There he learned the Arabic and decimal system of numbering. When he was 27 years old, he returned to Italy and published what became widely known as *Liber Abaci* (1202), in which he demonstrated the great advantage of the Arabic system of numeration as compared to the Roman (for instance, 98 instead of XCVIII).

THE FIBONACCI SUMMATION SERIES

Think of all the wonders in nature: oceans, trees, flowers, plant life, animals, and microorganisms. Think of all the achievements of humans in the natural sciences: medicine, nuclear theory, computer technology, radio, and television. And finally, think of the trend moves in the world markets. It may surprise you to know that all of these have one underlying pattern in common: the Fibonacci summation series.

The Fibonacci summation series is considered the most important mathematical representation of natural phenomena ever discovered. The series can be found in nature, geometry, and music. It is found in the logarithmic spiral, one of the most beautiful mathematical curves, which is seen in the nautilus shell, the snowflake, and the honeycomb. Ratios derived by the Fibonacci summation series create the dimensions of the "golden rectangle," which also happens to be the proportions of the Parthenon, the temple of Athena, in Athens.

Generally speaking, the Fibonacci summation series is nature's law, and it is a part of the aesthetic found in any kind of perfect shape or curve.

Fibonacci discovered how nature's law related to the summation series when he proposed that the progeny of a single pair of rabbits increased in a particular repeatable pattern:

Suppose there is one pair of rabbits in January, which then breed a second pair of rabbits in February, and, thereafter, these offspring produce another pair every month. The mathematical problem is to find how many pairs of rabbits we have at the end of December.

To solve this puzzle, we tabulate the data in four columns:

1. The total number of pairs of breeding rabbits at the beginning of each given month;

2. The total number of pairs of nonbreeding rabbits at the beginning of each month;

3. The total number of pairs of rabbits bred during each month;

4. The total number of pairs of rabbits living at the end of 12
months.

Question 1–1:
**Fill in Column (4) in Table 1.1 for the first six months and
then complete the whole table.**

Table 1.1   **Progeny of a Single Pair of Rabbits,
According to Fibonacci**

Month	(1)	(2)	(3)	(4)
January	0	1	0	?
February	1	0	1	?
March	1	1	1	?
April	2	1	2	?
May	3	2	3	?
June	5	3	5	?
July	?	?	?	?
August	?	?	?	?
September	?	?	?	?

After filling in the appropriate figures, readers should notice a
particular number pattern, and then consider the Fibonacci summation series, which is:

1, 1, 2, 3, 5, 8, 13, 21, 34, 55, 89 . . . , and so on ad infinitum.

By answering Questions 1–2 and 1–3, readers should be able to
see how the value of the Fibonacci summation series is manifested in
different ways.

Question 1–2:

Why are the stems and the flowers of the sneezewort, in Figure 1.1, a perfect example of the Fibonacci summation series in nature?

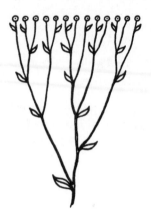

Figure 1.1   Fibonacci numbers found in the flowers of the sneezewort.

The sunflower has beautiful curving lines that have existed naturally for thousands of centuries in flora and fauna, and have been studied by mathematicians for hundreds of years.

The sunflower has two sets of equiangular spirals superimposed and intertwined, one turning clockwise and the other turning counterclockwise.

Question 1–3:

What does the scheme of a sunflower in Figure 1.2 have in common with the Fibonacci summation series?

Figure 1.2   Rule of alternation shown in the sunflower.

THE FIBONACCI RATIO IN NATURE AND GEOMETRY

Once again, the numbers of the Fibonacci summation series run as 1, 1, 2, 3, 5, 8, 13, 21, 34, 55, 89, 144, and so on.

While these numbers represent nature's law, the ratios derived by them are called the Fibonacci ratios. These ratios have an important impact in nature, geometry, and physics, and can also be found in the price patterns in futures, stock index futures, cash currencies, and stocks, as long as there is volatility. These ratios are used in all Fibonacci trading tools in this book and are, therefore, the link between the Fibonacci summation series and real-time trading.

Question 1–4:
How is the estimated ratio 1.618 calculated from the number sequence in the Fibonacci summation series?

Question 1–5:
How is the estimated ratio 0.618 calculated from the number sequence in the Fibonacci summation series?

Based on the Fibonacci ratios, we can interpret several natural phenomena in mathematical and geometric terms, such as golden rectangles, PHI-spirals, and PHI-ellipses.

Golden Section and Golden Rectangles

What we refer to as the Fibonacci ratio was originally called the "golden section."

The famous Greek mathematician, Euclid of Megara, (450 to 370 B.C.), was the first scientist to write about the golden section and to focus on the analysis of a straight line.

The golden section also interested mathematicians in the Middle Ages and during the Renaissance. In 1509, a dissertation titled *De Divina Proportione* was published by Luca Pacioli and was illustrated by Leonardo da Vinci. The dissertation explained that the golden section (as well as the golden rectangle) was very important in art. Paintings were not considered beautiful if the figures within a picture were not placed in the proportion of the golden section. Pacioli advised that figures should never be placed in the middle of a picture, but rather positioned so that the ratio of the short to the long side had the proportion of the Fibonacci ratio, 1.618.

The core structure of the geometry of a golden rectangle is shown in Figure 1.3.

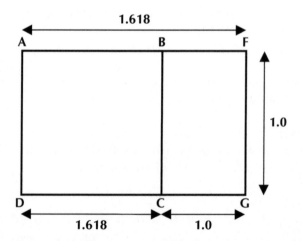

Figure 1.3   Geometry of a golden rectangle. *Source:* FAM Research, 2000.

Question 1–6:
How is the well-known Parthenon at Athens (Figure 1.4), built in the fifth century B.C., related to the Fibonacci ratio?

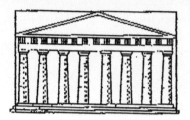

Figure 1.4 Parthenon temple in Athens.

PHI-Spirals

The PHI-spiral is considered the most beautiful of mathematical curves, and is also a type of magnificent trading tool, as we will show in Chapter 6.

We can apply PHI-spirals as Fibonacci trading devices to analyze stock, futures, and commodity markets.

Question 1–7:
How is the PHI-spiral in Figure 1.5 associated with the Fibonacci ratio 1.618 and the Fibonacci summation series?

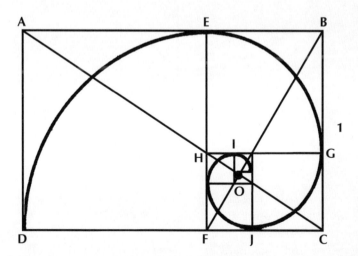

Figure 1.5 Geometry of a PHI-spiral. *Source:* FAM Research, 2000.

PHI-Ellipses

The PHI-ellipse is the mathematical expression of an oval. Each PHI-ellipse can be precisely designated by only a few characteristics.

Many of the natural curves can be geometrically modeled using ellipses. The most significant examples include the horizon of the ocean, the meteor track, the parabola of a waterfall, the arc the sun travels in the sky, the crescent of the moon, or the flight of a bird.

We will show, in Chapter 5, that the PHI-ellipse is one of the most important Fibonacci trading devices and can be used by making the shape of the PHI-ellipse thicker or thinner, longer or shorter, with the help of the Fibonacci ratios.

The basic geometric structure of PHI-ellipses is shown in Figure 1.6.

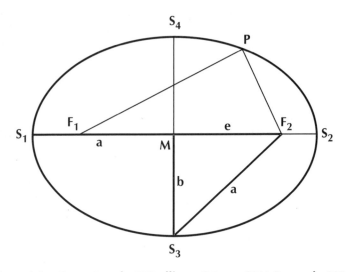

Figure 1.6   Geometry of a PHI-ellipse. *Source:* FAM Research, 2000.

THE ELLIOTT WAVE PRINCIPLE

Ralph Nelson Elliott (1871–1948) began his career as an engineer, not a professional analyst. Having recovered from a serious illness during the 1930s, he turned his focus of interest to the analysis of stock prices and became a specialist in analysis of the Dow-Jones Index.

Elliott based his discoveries on nature's law. He noted: "This law behind the market can only be discovered when the market is viewed in its proper light and then is analyzed from this approach. Simply put, the stock market is a creation of man and, therefore, reflects human idiosyncrasy." Elliott divided all human activities into three distinctive features: pattern, time, and ratio. All of these features abide by the Fibonacci summation series.

Question 1–8:
Based on what you have read so far in this workbook, which of these three features do you think Elliott considered the most important: pattern, time, or ratio?

Elliott described the market cycle as being divided primarily into a "bull market" and a "bear market," and as having waves of three types: major waves, intermediate waves, and minor waves (Figure 1.7).

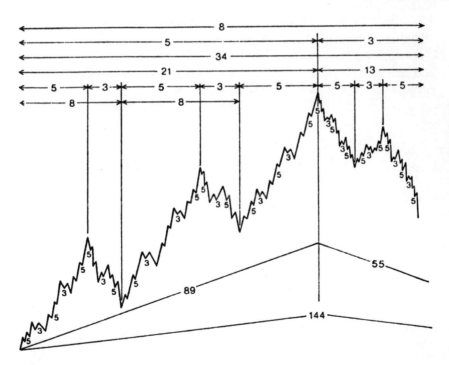

Figure 1.7   Elliott's perfect stock market cycle, consisting of major waves, intermediate waves, and minor waves. *Source: Fibonacci Applications and Strategies for Traders,* R. Fischer (New York: Wiley, 1993), p. 20.

A bull market, according to Elliott, can be divided into five major waves. A bear market can be divided into three major waves.

Each of the major waves 1, 3, and 5 of the bull market is subdivided into five intermediate waves. Then each of the intermediate waves 1, 3, and 5 is subdivided into five minor waves, which makes the stock market cycle "perfect."

Question 1–9:
Why do you think it might be difficult to apply Elliott's generalized market concept to real-time trading?

Three core elements can be found in Elliott's wave analysis of the markets: corrections, rule of alternation in wave patterns, and extensions.

Corrections

There is a series of market patterns that applies to almost every situation in market development.

Figure 1.8 shows four ideal types of corrective moves in the second and fourth waves in 3-wave and 5-wave patterns. (Patterns are reversed for trend moves to the downside.)

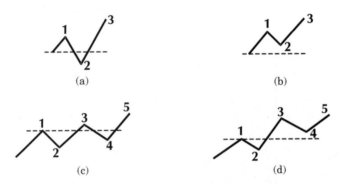

Figure 1.8   Alternative wave patterns in 3-wave and 5-wave trend upmoves.
Source: Fibonacci Applications and Strategies for Traders, R. Fischer (New York: Wiley, 1993), p. 14.

Elliott's wave principles of markets steadily moving in a wave rhythm are brilliantly conceived. The principles work perfectly in regular markets and give stunning results when looking back on charts, which means that wave 2 will not retrace to the beginning of wave 1, and wave 4 will not correct lower than the top of wave 1. This is the case in charts (b) and (d) of Figure 1.8.

Elliott admitted that there were other possibilities, as shown in charts (a) and (c) of Figure 1.8, but in these cases, the rules to analyze the markets would have to be adjusted.

Elliott's Rule of Alternation

One of Elliott's most important observations while analyzing corrections was the rule of alternation.

Based on this rule, Elliott connected the expression of natural human behavior to stock market swings (Figure 1.9).

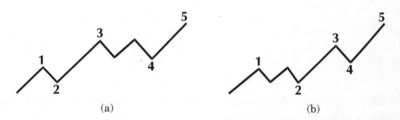

(a)   (b)

Figure 1.9 Simple waves and complex waves alternating. (a) Wave 4 is complex, wave 2 is simple; (b) wave 2 is complex, wave 4 is simple. *Source: Fibonacci Applications and Strategies for Traders,* R. Fischer (New York: Wiley, 1993), p. 14.

Following Elliott's concept, each of the corrective waves 2 and 4 can be subdivided into three waves of a smaller degree. The corrective waves 2 and 4 alternate in pattern. Elliott called this the rule of alternation.

If wave 2 is simple, wave 4 will be complex, and vice versa. Furthermore, wave 2 (or wave 4) consists of subwaves and does not go straight, as simple waves do.

With the remarkable observation that waves of the simple and the complex type alternate, and by formulating this as a rule for market development, Elliott linked nature's law to human behavior and thus to investors' behavior.

Extensions

Elliott sought solutions not only for market corrections (corrective waves), but also for impulse waves, which, many times, have erratic, fast price moves. Elliott called these erratic, fast price moves "extensions."

Extensions can occur in waves 1, 3, and 5 of five-wave price moves. The three different price patterns of extensions are shown in Figure 1.10.

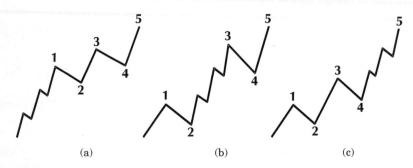

Figure 1.10 (a) First wave extension in an uptrend; (b) third wave extension in an uptrend; (c) fifth wave extension in an uptrend. *Source: Fibonacci Applications and Strategies for Traders,* R. Fischer (New York: Wiley, 1993), p. 17.

Elliott analyzed extensions as reinforcements of trends (whether uptrends or downtrends) to either side of the market. He wrote: "Extensions may appear in any one of the three impulse waves, wave 1, 3, or 5, but never in more than one."

GEOMETRIC FIBONACCI TRADING TOOLS

The final section of this introductory chapter is designed to give readers an overview of the six Fibonacci trading tools that form the backbone of our Fibonacci analysis.

All six Fibonacci tools are based on pattern recognition and can be applied by investors to real-time analysis and to trading the markets. The two questions added to Trading Tool 3 will familiarize readers with the devices described in detail in the upcoming chapters.

Trading Tool 1: Fibonacci Summation Series

It might be astonishing at first, but the Fibonacci summation series is easily turned into a trading tool for market analysis that works in a stable and reliable manner.

Following Elliott's discoveries, a price move in a particular market direction should continue up to a point where figures of the Fibonacci summation series—1, 1, 2, 3, 5, 8, 13, 21, 34, 55, 89, 144, . . .—are completed. For example, a price move that exceeds 13 days should continue to the next number of 21 days, and a price move that exceeds 21 days should continue to the next number of 34 days, and so on.

Therefore, the figures of the Fibonacci summation series can be integrated into Elliott's perfect stock market cycle, as we have already seen in Figure 1.7.

This basic method of calculating trend changes may be applied just as successfully on hourly, daily, weekly, or monthly data. But this is only an ideal type of pattern, and traders must never expect commodities, futures, stock index futures, or stocks to behave in such a precise and predictable manner. Deviations can and will occur, both in time and in amplitude, because individual waves and price patterns are not always likely to develop in a regular way. In addition, the number of bars in sideward markets remains unpredictable.

Trading Tool 2: Fibonacci Time-Goal Analysis

Our time analysis is based on the important findings of Euclid of Megara and his invention of the golden section, discussed earlier.

We link nature's law, expressed in mathematical terms through the Fibonacci ratio PHI = 1.618, to market swings in a way that can be graphically illustrated (see Figure 1.11).

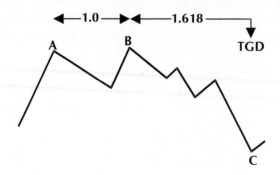

Figure 1.11 Calculation of Fibonacci time-goal days (TGD). *Source:* FAM Research, 2000.

Measuring the distance from peak A and peak B in days (or whatever time unit is chosen), we can multiply this distance by the Fibonacci ratio PHI = 1.618 to forecast the resulting point C, which is designated the Fibonacci time-goal day.

A forecast of Fibonacci time-goal days will not indicate whether the price will be high or low on a particular day. It can be either. The time-goal day only forecasts a trend change (a simple event) at the time the goal is reached, but does not tell the direction of the event.

Trading Tool 3: Corrections and Extensions

The most common approach to working with corrections is to relate the size of the correction to a percentage of a prior impulse market move.

Any correction can (percentagewise) be a retracement of up to 100.0% of the original price move at the beginning of the impulse wave. If a price move goes below the value at the start of the previous impulse wave, we usually will not have to consider a correction any longer. Instead, we must look for the beginning of a new impulse wave in the opposite market direction.

In our analysis, we focus on the three most prominent percentage values of possible market corrections. These can be directly derived from the quotients of the PHI series and the Fibonacci sequence:

1. 38.2% is the result of the division 0.618 ÷ 1.618;

2. 50.0% is the transformed ratio 1.000;

3. 61.8% is the result of the immediate ratio 1.000 ÷ 1.618.

Question 1–10:
In Figure 1.12, how far would a retracement of 38.2%, 50.0%, and 61.8% correct the preceding impulse wave?

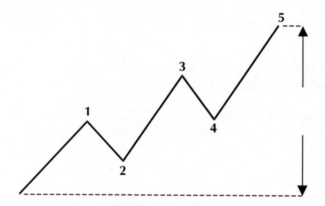

Figure 1.12   Correction levels after a 5-wave trend move.

Question 1–11:
Extensions, in contrast to corrections, are exuberant price movements. They express themselves in runaway markets, opening gaps, limit-up and limit-down price moves, and

high volatility. What PHI ratios are we using in calculating extensions, and how are these PHI ratios used in Figure 1.13?

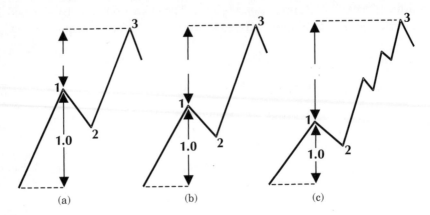

Figure 1.13   Extensions in the third wave of a trend move. *Source:* FAM Research, 2000.

Trading Tool 4: PHI-Channels

The general idea behind PHI-channels as Fibonacci-related trading devices becomes clear when Figure 1.14 is studied.

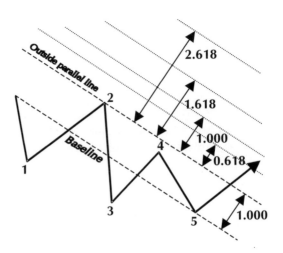

Figure 1.14   PHI-channel. *Source:* FAM Research, 2000.

The width of the PHI-channel is calculated as the distance between the baseline and the outside parallel line. This distance is set to 1.000. Parallel lines are then drawn in PHI-series distances starting with 0.618 times the size of the channel and continuing at 1.000 times, 1.618 times, 2.618 times, and so on, to the width of the PHI-channel.

Trading Tool 5: PHI-Spirals

PHI-spirals are the perfect geometric approximations of nature's law and natural growth. As the PHI-spiral grows, it increases by a constant ratio 1.618 with every full cycle.

Figure 1.15 shows, in a schematic way, the process of growth of a PHI-spiral.

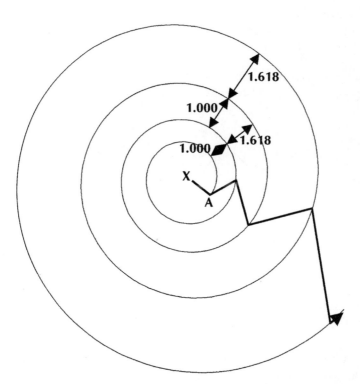

Figure 1.15   PHI-spiral. *Source:* FAM Research, 2000.

The PHI-spiral represents an optimal combination of price and time. Corrections and trend changes occur at all those prominent points where the PHI-spiral is touched on its growth path through price and time. Using PHI-spirals as Fibonacci tools, we discover a stunning symmetry in the price pattern of charts, whether it represents weekly, daily, or intraday stocks; cash currencies; futures; or commodities. The stronger the behavioral pattern becomes in extreme market conditions, the better PHI-spirals work to inform investors **in advance** about tops and bottoms of market moves.

Trading Tool 6: PHI-Ellipses

In this tool, we present a PHI-ellipse as a Fibonacci trading device; we have transformed the underlying mathematical formula that describes the shape of the regular ellipse.

With each increasing Fibonacci number, a regular ellipse turns very quickly into a "Havana cigar" (it becomes very thin). Our Fischer-transformed PHI-ellipse holds its shape much longer and is, therefore, better for analyzing price data (Figure 1.16).

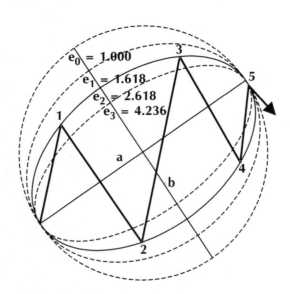

**Figure 1.16   Fischer-transformed PHI-ellipses; $e_x = (a \div b)^*$. *Source:* FAM Research, 2000.

What makes the PHI-ellipse distinct from any other trading tool? It circumvents price moves. In Chapter 5, we will show that a price move often stays within the correctly chosen PHI-ellipse and gives very reliable trading signals, especially when used in connection with other Fibonacci trading tools.

ANSWERS TO QUESTIONS

This chapter has introduced a wide spectrum of how the Fibonacci principles can be understood, but it is still a very small portion of what is covered in the book.

The answers to the questions in this chapter cover as much information as is possible about the specific subjects raised. They are explained in much more detail on pages 1 to 36 of the textbook.

Answer to Question 1–1:

Table 1.2 shows the correct completion of the columns in Table 1.1. The progeny of a single pair of rabbits over the months is:

Table 1.2 Progeny of a Single Pair of Rabbits, According to Fibonacci

Month	(1)	(2)	(3)	(4)
January	0	1	0	1
February	1	0	1	2
March	1	1	1	3
April	2	1	2	5
May	3	2	3	8
June	5	3	5	13
July	8	5	8	21
August	13	8	13	34
September	21	13	21	55

Each column contains Fibonacci's summation series, formed according to the rule that any number is the sum of the pair of immediately preceding numbers.

Answer to Question 1–2:

The sneezewort is an ideal example of Fibonacci's summation series in nature, for every new branch springs from the axil and more branches grow from a new branch. Adding the old and the new branches together, a Fibonacci number is found in each horizontal plane.

Answer to Question 1–3:

The fascinating combination of spirals in the sunflower shows that the numbers of spirals are closely related to the Fibonacci summation series. There are 21 clockwise and 34 counterclockwise spirals. The order of spirals is closely related to the rule of alternation, which Elliott used in his wave principles to explain human behavior.

Answer to Question 1–4:

If each number that is part of the Fibonacci summation series is divided by its preceding value (e.g., $13 \div 8$ or $21 \div 13$), the operation results in a ratio that oscillates around the irrational figure 1.618, being higher than the ratio one time, and lower the next. The precise ratio will never be known to the last digit. We will refer to the Fibonacci ratio as 1.618 and ask the reader to keep the margin of error in mind.

Answer to Question 1–5:

Dividing any number of the Fibonacci summation series by the following number (e.g., $8 \div 13$ or $13 \div 21$), we find that the series asymptotically gets closer to the ratio 0.618.

Answer to Question 1–6:

The proportion of the well-known Parthenon temple in Athens bears witness to the influence exerted by the golden rectangle on Greek architecture.

The proportion of the Parthenon temple fits exactly into a golden rectangle; the total width of the Parthenon is exactly 1.618 times its total height.

Answer to Question 1–7:

The quotient of the length and height of rectangle ABCD in Figure 1.5 can be calculated by AB ÷ BC = PHI ÷ 1 = 1.618. Through point E, also called the golden cut of AB, line EF is drawn perpendicular to AB, cutting the square, AEFD, from the rectangle. The remaining rectangle, EBCF, is a golden rectangle. If the square, EBGH, is isolated, the then remaining figure, HGCF, is also a golden rectangle. This process can be repeated indefinitely until the limiting rectangle O is so small that it is indistinguishable from a point. The limiting point O is called the pole of the equal angle spiral, which passes through the golden cuts D, E, G, J, and so on. The sides of the rectangle are nearly, but not completely, tangential to the curve.

The relation of the PHI-spiral to the Fibonacci series is evident from Figure 1.5. The PHI-spiral passes diagonally through opposite corners of successive squares, such as DE, EG, GJ, and so on. The lengths of the sides of these squares form a Fibonacci series. If the smallest square has a side of length d, the adjacent square must also have a side of length d. The next square has a side of length 2d (twice as long as d), the next of 3d (three times the length of d), forming the series 1d, 2d, 3d, 5d, 8d, 13d, . . . which is exactly the well-known Fibonacci sequence 1–1–2–3–5–8–13– and so on, indefinitely.

The PHI-spiral is the link between the Fibonacci summation series, the resulting Fibonacci ratio PHI, and the magic of nature that we enjoy all around us.

Answer to Question 1–8:

In Elliott's opinion, the most important of the three factors is pattern. A pattern is permanently in progress, repeated over and over again. Usually, but not invariably, one can see in advance the appropriate type of pattern.

We do not agree with Elliott in this respect. In our opinion, the Fibonacci ratio, which Elliott worked with, is the most important of the three factors. Without this ratio, none of our trading tools would work.

Answer to Question 1-9:

The problem with Elliott's general market concept is that, most of the time, there are no regular 5-wave swings. The regular 5-wave swing is only the exception to a rule. Elliott tried to fine-tune it by introducing a sophisticated variation of the concept. In most cases, the market price does not complete the 5-wave cycle.

The complex nature of Elliott's wave structure does not leave room for forecasts of future price moves in advance. The schemes and the structures look perfect in retrospect. The multitude of rules and situations described by Elliott can be well used to fit any price pattern after the fact. But that is not good enough for real-time trading.

Answer to Question 1-10:

We focus on the three most prominent percentage values of possible market corrections: 38.2%, 50.0%, and 61.8%. These values are directly derived from the Fibonacci sequence and the quotients of the PHI series. We integrate these ratios into a chart, to calculate the retracement levels.

Figure 1.17 shows the results of our calculation of correction levels based on a 5-wave impulse swing.

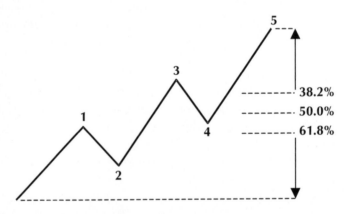

Figure 1.17 Correction levels of 38.2%, 50.0%, and 61.8% after a 5-wave trend move to the upside. *Source: Fibonacci Applications and Strategies for Traders,* R. Fischer (New York: Wiley, 1993), p. 52.

Answer to Question 1–11:

If we relate the PHI ratios 0.618, 1.000, and 1.618 to a percentage of a prior impulse market move, we are able to calculate different levels of extensions to define price targets for turning points in the markets.

Figure 1.18 illustrates combinations of the ratios 0.618, 1.000, and 1.618 with respective impulse moves.

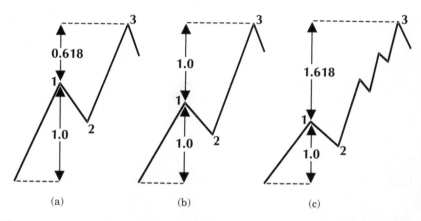

(a)   (b)   (c)

Figure 1.18 Extensions in the third wave of a trend, and the Fibonacci ratio PHI: (a) ratio 0.618; (b) ratio 1.000; (c) ratio 1.618. *Source: Fibonacci Applications and Strategies for Traders,* R. Fischer (New York: Wiley, 1993), p. 52.

FINAL REMARKS

The first chapter of this workbook was intended to be fun to read and educational, to show readers how Elliott's wave principles fit into the Fibonacci summation series, and how the powerful Fibonacci ratios are part of nature and geometry and have fascinated people for thousands of years.

Whether one is a professional or a novice, the most important part of working with geometric Fibonacci trading tools is to believe in the underlying power of nature's law and natural patterns.

Once it is understood that the Fibonacci ratios are not a one-time event, but an ongoing process that repeats itself over and over again, working with geometric Fibonacci trading tools becomes much easier.

Each Fibonacci tool explained in the following chapters can be traded individually, but the most powerful signals can be seen when several Fibonacci tools pinpoint the same significant turning point in the markets.

The final chapter of this workbook will show readers how the combination of different Fibonacci trading devices can be mastered.

2

APPLYING THE FIBONACCI SUMMATION SERIES

The Fibonacci summation series is the basis for all six trading tools presented in this workbook. Therefore, Chapter 2 centers on patterns and chart analysis, for which we need no special tools other than the Fibonacci sequence. We begin by focusing on this series to show the rhythm of price swings and the opportunities for combining that rhythm with other trading tools.

We will first concentrate on how to link the Fibonacci summation series to Elliott's wave principles. Then we will show how to apply these concepts to daily data. For both analytical steps, we present questions and exercises.

BASIC PRINCIPLES OF APPLICATION

When applying our geometric Fibonacci concepts to actual trading, we always return to the numbers in the Fibonacci summation series:

1, 1, 2, 3, 5, 8, 13, 21, 34, 55, 89, 144, and so on.

The values of the Fibonacci summation series can be linked to Elliott's method of counting waves in market price patterns (see Figure 2.1).

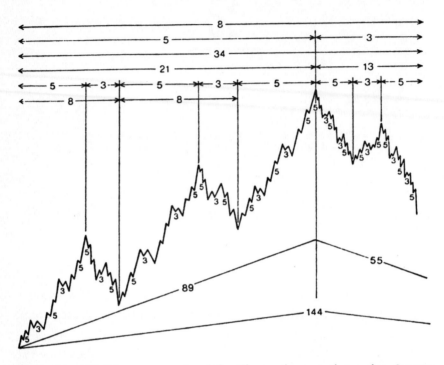

Figure 2.1   Elliott's wave count and the Fibonacci summation series. *Source: Fibonacci Applications and Strategies for Traders,* R. Fischer (New York: Wiley, 1993), p. 20.

If we combine the numbers of the Fibonacci summation series with the findings of Elliott, we can count out Elliott's waves in the first bull-market cycle seen in Figure 2.1:

$$5 + 3 + 5 + 3 + 5 = 21$$

21 is a number in the Fibonacci summation series. In fact, the chart shows all the numbers of the Fibonacci summation series in Elliott's complete market cycle: 3, 5, 8, 13, 21, 34, 55, 89, and 144.

One might wonder what the practical value of these numbers will be in actual trading. The core principle is that a move in a particular direction should continue up to a point where a time frame—part of and consistent with the Fibonacci summation series—is completed. Our experience shows that the smallest number to work with from the Fibonacci summation series is 8. A move that extends itself beyond 8 days should not reverse until 13 days are reached. A move over 13 days should extend itself to 21 days, and so on.

This does not mean that trend changes will always occur at the precalculated points (8, 13, 21, 34, 55, . . .), but research shows that it happens too often to be ignored.

PRACTICAL APPLICATION

As we will see in the practical examples, the most effective ways to work with the Fibonacci summation series numbers are: (1) to designate where different time-goal days from different starting points converge, and (2) to apply the numbers to other Fibonacci trading devices. These applications will be described herein.

Traders who follow the methods of Elliott calculate major trend changes in the cash currencies, commodities, futures, or stock markets by applying the numbers of the Fibonacci summation series to monthly and yearly data. This may make sense conceptually, but it is of very little value if the turning points are years ahead of time. Traders want results instantly, or, at the most, a couple of weeks ahead of time.

Question 2–1:
Why should the numbers of the Fibonacci summation series not be applied to intraday data?

Question 2–2:
Why is the Fibonacci summation series most effective as an analytic tool on widely used products such as the S&P500 Index, the DAX30 Index, cash currencies, or stocks with a very large capitalization?

Confirmations

Confirmations of a trend change can make trading much safer and more profitable.

The confirmation of a peak/valley based on chart patterns will show that the momentum of the price move has changed, but this is a "lagging indicator."

The confirmation of a trend change by two or more numbers out of the Fibonacci summation series indicates a price change in the future and is a "leading indicator."

Peaks and valleys can be confirmed with either a chart pattern or a swing size. Both opportunities are addressed in the pair of questions that follows.

Question 2–3:
We start counting the number of days of the Fibonacci summation series from significant peaks and valleys. What is an example of a chart pattern that could confirm a significant peak or valley?

Question 2–4:
Another way to confirm a significant peak or valley is with swing size. If we want to confirm the high of a peak, and the given swing size is a minimum of 100 basis points, at what price level is the peak confirmed at the end of the trading day when we start measuring from the highest high?

(a) **The close of any following day is equal to or more than 100 basis points below the highest high.**

(b) **The high of any following day is equal to or lower than 100 basis points lower than the highest high.**

(c) **The low of any following day is equal to or more than 100 basis points below the highest high.**

Peak/Valley Confirmations with Overlapping Time Targets

The lagging indicator of the chart pattern tells us that the momentum of a price move might have changed. We work with time targets because we want to forecast when a trend might have changed its direction.

Although the distance of 8, 13, 21, 34, or 55 days (or weeks) is counted from every peak or valley, we use only those counts that are equal or overlap, and are thereby multiples of other counts (Figure 2.2).

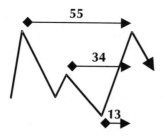

Figure 2.2   Confirmation of a peak by multiple Fibonacci numbers. *Source: FAM Research, 2000.*

If, for instance, we count 34 days from a peak, and this precalculated time is not confirmed with another count of 8, 13, 21, 34, or 55 days (or weeks) from any other confirmed peak or valley, we ignore this count.

Question 2–5:
When we are confirming a trend change, why do we require the overlap of multiple time targets calculated from different peaks or valleys with numbers out of the Fibonacci summation series?

Time Bands

The counts from different highs and lows with different numbers of the Fibonacci summation series do not always match the same day when looking for a trend change, and there is often a time band between different counts.

We have established that, to be acceptable and to confirm a peak or valley, a time band should not be wider than four days (Figure 2.3).

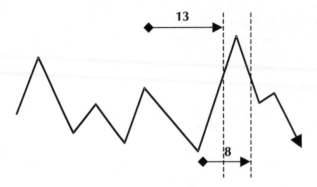

Figure 2.3   Confirmation of a peak by numbers of the Fibonacci summation series in a time band. *Source:* FAM Research, 2000.

Question 2–6:
What might be the reason that time goals calculated from different highs or lows with different numbers of the Fibonacci summation series do not completely overlap?

From the presentation of peak/valley confirmations and time bands as important general factors, we can proceed to the application of the Fibonacci counts to market data.

Application to the S&P500 Index

Stock index futures are very liquid trading vehicles with clear peak/valley formations at appropriate swing sizes. We use daily data of the S&P500 Index for many of our examples, because this product has the volatility and market participation necessary to apply the Fibonacci trading tools. Other indexes that work equally well include the German DAX30 Index, Japan's NIKKEI Index, or Hong Kong's HANGSENG Index.

Exercise 2–A will allow readers to practice applying the Fibonacci summation series to market data. The exercise will be based on Figure 2.4.

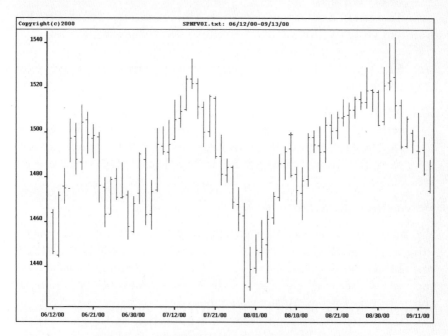

Figure 2.4   S&P500 Index from 06–00 to 09–00.

We will use the following parameters:

- Numbers from the Fibonacci summation series: 8, 13, 21, 34, and 55, counted only from major peaks or valleys;

- Swing size of 50 basis points;

- For a peak: At least two closing prices, on either side of the day with the highest high, that are lower than the low of the highest-high day (vice versa for a valley);

- Or, alternatively for a peak: Two closing prices that are lower than the close of the highest-high day (vice versa for a valley);

- Holidays are not skipped; they are counted as regular trading days.

Exercise 2–A:
To learn how to work with the numbers from the Fibonacci summation series, complete the following steps:

(a) **In Figure 2.4, mark the significant peaks and valleys on the basis of the given parameters.**

(b) **After the significant highs and lows are identified, count with the numbers from the Fibonacci summation series (8, 13, 21, 34, and 55), and indicate the time bands necessary for identifying peaks and valleys in the same chart.**

Application to the Japanese Yen Cash Currency

We can use the Japanese Yen cash currency versus the US Dollar as an example, because, like many stock index futures, it has the volatility and market participation needed for application of the Fibonacci trading tools. Other cash currencies—the Euro against the US Dollar, or the cross-rate Euro against the Japanese Yen—work equally well.

Cash currencies, as a product, are interesting to trade (a) because of their volatility and (b) because they trade 24 hours daily from Monday to Friday.

To analyze daily data on the Japanese Yen cash currency, we proceed in the same way as with the S&P500 Index. We use the same rules to determine peaks and valleys, and, again, we count the Fibonacci figures (8, 13, 21, 34, and 55) only from major peaks and major valleys.

The swing size for valid peaks and valleys has to be a minimum of 150 Japanese Yen cash currency ticks (e.g., from 108.00 to 109.50). Holidays are counted as regular trading days.

Figure 2.5 is a chart of the Japanese Yen cash currency for the period from June 2000 to October 2000.

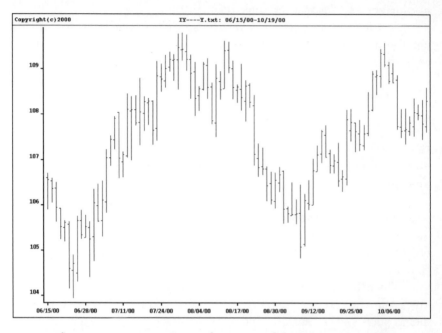

Figure 2.5   Japanese Yen cash currency from 06–00 to 10–00.

Exercise 2–B:
To learn how to work with the numbers from the Fibonacci summation series, complete the following steps:

(a) **In Figure 2.5, mark the significant peaks and valleys on the basis of the given parameters.**

(b) **When the significant highs and lows have been identified, use the numbers from the Fibonacci summation series (8, 13, 21, 34, and 55), and locate the time bands necessary for identifying peaks or valleys in the same chart.**

ANSWERS TO QUESTIONS AND EXERCISES

In this chapter, we have introduced the numbers of the Fibonacci summation series as a trading tool.

The following answers cover the specific subjects raised in this chapter's questions and exercises. For a more detailed explanation, consult the textbook.

Answer to Question 2–1:

For intraday data, the numbers of the Fibonacci summation series are of very little value. Markets that are extended sideward, or that exhibit much more erratic moves during the trading day make it almost impossible to use the Fibonacci figures intraday for serious analysis.

Answer to Question 2–2:

If the figures of the Fibonacci summation series represent nature's law, then human behavior must also be expressed in these figures.

The effects of human behavior are evident in market pricing at any given time. It is obvious that liquidity and heavily traded instruments such as the S&P500 Index or the Japanese Yen cash currency are better indicators of human behavior than niche products like futures contracts on pork bellies or lumber. The Fibonacci summation series may still work on these products, but not as accurately.

Answer to Question 2–3:

A significant peak (or significant valley) is confirmed when we have, for instance, at least two closing prices on either side of the day with a highest high that is lower than the low of the highest day, or two closing prices that are lower than the close of the highest day (Figure 2.6).

(a)   (b)

Figure 2.6 Swing high formations based on (a) the low of the highest day and (b) the close of the highest day. *Source:* **FAM Research, 2000.**

These two formations are not the only chart patterns that can be used to confirm a trend change. Another confirmation of a peak occurs when we have three lows that are lower than the closing price of the highest day (vice versa for the confirmation of a significant valley).

The choice depends on the risk preference of the investor. Does he feel more comfortable with a chart pattern of faster or of slower speed? We recommend using a medium speed.

Answer to Question 2–4:

If we want to confirm the high of a peak, and the given swing size is a minimum of 100 basis points, we have to start measuring the swing size from the highest high to the low of any following day. If the low is equal to or more than 100 basis points below the highest high, the peak is confirmed.

Answer to Question 2–5:

On daily data, two or more Fibonacci counts calculated from different peaks or valleys give a stronger indication for a trend change than if we have only one Fibonacci count. Looking for multiple numbers also will eliminate many of the single counts and make it easier to distinguish relatively safe trend changes.

Answer to Question 2–6:

The time goals do not completely overlap because price targets and time targets calculated with different Fibonacci tools do not overlap (Figure 2.7).

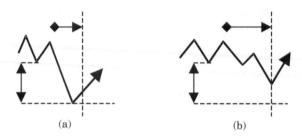

(a)   (b)

Figure 2.7 Dominance of (a) price goal and (b) time goal. *Source:* FAM Research, 2000.

In case (a) in Figure 2.7, the price goal is reached before the time goal. In case (b), the time goal is reached before the price goal. There is no way to determine, in advance, whether price or time targets are more important for a price move.

In Chapter 8, we will discuss how to work with multiple Fibonacci tools in more detail.

Exercise 2–A:

The parameters for the analysis are described on pages 31–32 and are clear regarding the definitions of peaks and valleys, as well as the confirmations of major highs and lows by multiple counts from the Fibonacci summation series.

In Exercise 2–A, we only show the counts that result in the confirmation of peaks and valleys. Counts for peaks and valleys are omitted where an insufficient number of days is available to complete one Fibonacci count. Invalid counts occur when counts are not confirmed by overlapping Fibonacci numbers.

Eight turning points in the S&P500 Index between June and September 2000 can be derived from calculations on Figure 2.8.

A peak (#6) and a valley (#7) are marked, although the swing size is not 50 basis points. The reason is that a smaller swing size is used if it is within 14 days from a significant peak or valley and the market price did not show a regular swing size (in this case, 50 basis points). This rule is explained in more detail in the textbook.

Figure 2.8 illustrates the market move in the S&P500 Index with Fibonacci counts added. Table 2.1 lists the characteristics of each turning point.

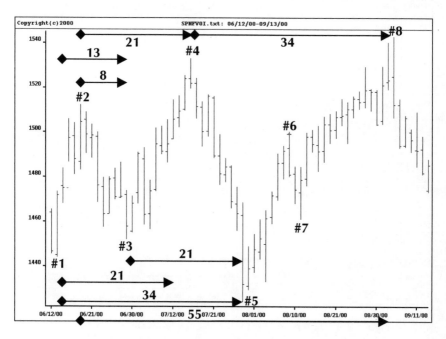

Figure 2.8   S&P500 Index from 06–00 to 09–00.

Table 2.1   Characteristics of Each Turning Point

Turning Point	Type	Initiation	Reference	Type
#3	Valley	8 Days	After #2	High
		13 Days	After #1	Low
#4	Peak	21 Days	After #2	High
		21 Days	After #1	Low
#5	Valley	21 Days	After #3	Low
		34 Days	After #1	Low
#8	Peak	34 Days	After #4	High
		55 Days	After #2	High

Exercise 2–B:

The parameters for analysis are described on pages 31–32. Figure 2.9 shows significant trend changes based on swing highs and swing lows in the Japanese Yen cash currency. Table 2.2 lists the characteristics of each turning point.

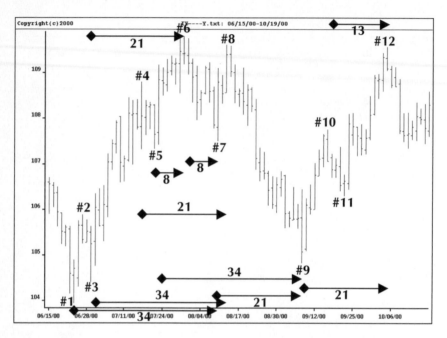

Figure 2.9   Japanese Yen cash currency from 06–00 to 10–00.

Table 2.2   Characteristics of Each Turning Point

Turning Point	Type	Initiation	Reference	Type
#6	Peak	8 Days	After #5	Low
		21 Days	After #3	Low
#7	Valley	8 Days	After #6	High
		34 Days	After #1	Low
#8	Peak	21 Days	After #4	High
		34 Days	After #3	Low
#9	Valley	21 Days	After #7	Low
		34 Days	After #5	Low
#12	Peak	13 Days	After #10	High
		21 Days	After #9	Low

With the Japanese Yen cash currency, the general parameters we apply for our analysis do not differ much from the parameters used with the S&P500 Index.

There is a total of 12 turning points in the chart of the Japanese Yen cash currency between June and October 2000. Peaks #2, #4, and #10, as well as valleys #1, #3, #5, and #11 are not shown as trend changes in the table, because of a lack of overlapping numbers of the Fibonacci summation series.

We do not show examples with weekly data. The only major modification in parameters would be that we no longer exclude those highs and lows that are designated by no more than one valid Fibonacci count.

Examples for the weekly analysis can be found in the textbook (pages 75–79).

FINAL REMARKS

The Fibonacci summation series is, by itself, a very powerful analytic tool for forecasting price changes.

By counting peaks and valleys with regard to a certain swing size, and by observing only the important figures (8, 13, 21, 34, 55), the Fibonacci summation series can be successfully applied to any product or any market. The more investors who participate in market action and the higher the liquidity and volatility in a market, the greater the potential of correctly forecasting turning points in the respective market.

The Fibonacci summation series and the Fibonacci ratios are expected to work best on market price data related to stock market indexes, index futures, cash currencies, or large-cap stocks worldwide, since investors' behavior is most concentrated in these types of liquid trading vehicles.

In daily analysis, we look for multiple confirmations of swing highs and swing lows by a minimum of two figures from the Fibonacci summation series. When dealing with weekly data, we work with single figures from the Fibonacci summation series because the weekly data work in our favor as a filter. Having Fibonacci numbers on weekly charts is even better for our peak and/or valley confirmation. We then look for the trend reversal, once the first number from the Fibonacci summation series is passed.

As we will see in later chapters, figures from the Fibonacci summation series can be easily combined with other geometric Fibonacci trading devices. The effect of different Fibonacci tools must be considered when analyzing why time bands have emerged or why price or time goals were not reached. In the final chapter of this book, we will show that a solid combination of tools should be the goal of every skillful trader who considers the Fibonacci method to be an effective and profitable means of investment.

Trend changes can only indicate the best time to trade in a market—long, short, or flat. We do not introduce a trading model here, but should a trader use this strategy for trading, entry rules and stop-loss rules must be integrated. The Fibonacci summation series can also be used profitably for strategic decisions such as asset allocation or position management in a portfolio.

The trading concept as a whole is available on the Internet, for registered members, at **www.fibotrader.com.** Data and software are continuously updated and upgraded.

3

Applying the Fibonacci Ratio to Corrections and Extensions

Markets move in rhythms. This is the main conclusion drawn from our introductory analysis of Elliott's basic theory.

An impulse wave that defines a major market trend will have a corrective wave before the next impulse wave reaches new territory. This occurs either in bull market or bear market conditions.

Extensions, in contrast to corrections, are exuberant price movements. They express themselves in runaway markets, opening gaps, limit-up and limit-down moves, and high volatility. These situations may offer extraordinary trading potential as long as the analysis is carried out in accordance with sensible and definite rules.

CORRECTIONS

Corrections and extensions can serve as powerful trading tools if the correct link to the Fibonacci summation series and the corresponding Fibonacci ratio PHI are established.

In this section, we will explain how corrections can be used as trading tools. Corrections will be linked to the Fibonacci ratio in principle, and will then be applied as charting tools to sets of daily and weekly data of various products.

Analysis would be easy if we were able to detect one general pattern of corrections. The problem is, when working with corrections, we can have more price patterns (in commodities, futures, stocks, or cash currencies) than impulse waves. The markets then move sideways for longer periods of time before a new impulse wave appears.

We can never predict which of the next waves will be an impulse wave instead of another false move in continuation of a sideways market. Markets are in a sideways condition about 70% of the time, and in a trending state only about 30% of the time. Therefore, every serious trading approach using corrections has to be designed to survive even the largest sideways market correction phase. There is no market pattern that can ensure us a profitable trade, for, at any given time, we might be in a correction of an impulse wave or at the beginning of a new impulse wave.

Whenever we work with corrections as an investment strategy, we must always work with stop-loss rules, profit target rules, and entry rules. This is very important, for we can only realize profit if the stop-loss is smaller than the profit targets and the number of profitable trades is higher than the number of losing trades. This strategy can be easily programmed and computerized, and the profit-loss profile of the specified parameters can be tested on historical data.

Basic Features of Corrections

Working with corrections is a trend-following strategy. It is based on the assumption that after a correction of an impulse wave up or down, the next impulse wave will follow in the direction of the first wave. In many cases, this assumption is correct; therefore, we consider working with corrections a valid investment strategy according to Fibonacci principles.

Working with corrections, however, is a short-term strategy. The main objective is to take small profits with a high number of profitable trades and small losses.

Traders must always be aware of the appearance of what Elliott called irregular tops or irregular bottoms. These market patterns are also called "bull traps" on the upside and "bear traps" on the downside, and are frequently seen, especially when working with intraday data.

Exercise 3–A:
Complete the charts in Figure 3.1 with a false breakout on the upside and a false breakout on the downside.

(a)   (b)

Figure 3.1   (a) False breakout to the upside; (b) false breakout to the downside.

Corrections and the Fibonacci ratio PHI are closely connected through the swing size and the volatility of a product. There is no standard rule as to what correction level will work best, although the kind of data compression used will make a big difference. The safest way to work with corrections is to test chosen products and strategies on historical data, using a computer program. In this chapter, we will give the reader guidelines and will show what we consider a prudent approach to working with corrections.

Size of Corrections

The most common approach to working with corrections as trading tools in research and practice is to relate the size of a correction to a percentage of a prior impulse move.

In our analysis, we focus on the three most prominent percentage values of possible market corrections. These can be directly derived from the quotients of the PHI series and the Fibonacci summation series:

- A retracement level of 38.2% is the result of the division of 0.618 ÷ 1.618;

- A retracement level of 50.0% is the transformed Fibonacci ratio 1.000;

- A retracement level of 61.8% is the result of the immediate ratio 1.000 ÷ 1.618.

Forecasting the exact size of a correction is an empirical problem. Investing after a correction of just 38.2% might be too early, and waiting for a correction of 61.8% might result in missing strong trends completely.

Question 3–1:
A handful of conditions affect safe investments in corrections. Some are out of traders' control, but most are conscious choices. What do you think are some of the most important ones?

The best way to establish a strong position in a correction is to create a sophisticated combination of the percentage of a correction and the swing size as a second parameter.

When working with corrections, we must identify the typical swing size of the product from which we wish to measure the corrections. Each product in any compression has an individual pattern that is best seen in historical test runs.

The swing size is a continued price move of the market in one direction. Each product moves up and down in bigger or smaller swings. It is necessary to decrease the "noise" by eliminating small movements that are not typical of a particular product.

Question 3–2:

**Consider the following price swing. How can we elimi-
nate the two minor moves to the downside in Figure 3.2?**

Figure 3.2   Sample market move of five days without filter. *Source:* FAM Research, 2000.

Entry Rules

Each product analyzed for market swings has an individual swing size. This is very important to understand because if we look at the Japanese Yen cash currency, a swing size of 200 basis points can occur in volatile markets once or twice a week, and might be too small to work with when using correction levels of 38.2%, 50.0%, or 61.8%. On the other hand, a 38.2% level might be very large when analyzed in combination with a minimum swing size of 1,000 basis points. It might take weeks before the market price has a correction of 382 basis points (which equals 38.2%).

It is risky to work with a market correction percentage of just 38.2%. The market might be entered too early, and the trader will get stopped out too many times. Waiting for a larger 61.2% correction might be too long, however, and if the market price does not reach our retracement level, we will miss the entire impulse wave for which we were waiting.

The reason for applying entry rules is to gain additional confirmations of a trend reversal. This approach is a compromise; using entry rules means that we will always enter a market later than if we worked outright with the plain correction target. Giving up profit potential is exchanged for protection against frequent whipsawing.

Table 3.1 shows variations and combinations of swing sizes, percentages of corrections, and entry rules.

Table 3.1 Swing Sizes, Corrections, and Entry Rules

Swing Sizes in Ticks	Corrections	Entry Rules: Previous High–Low in Days
100–200	61.8%	3–4
200–400	38.2	3–4
200–400	50.0	2
200–400	61.8	1
400–800	38.2	3
400–800	50.0	1
400–800	61.8	1

Source: FAM Research, 2000.

Entry rules in relation to different swing sizes and sizes of corrections are shown in Figure 3.3.

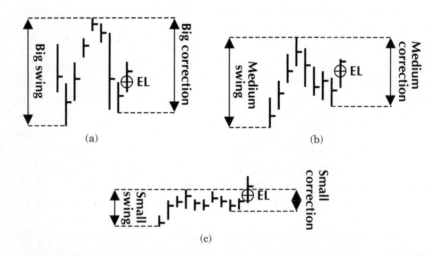

Figure 3.3 Swing sizes, correction levels, and entry rules. *Source: Fibonacci Applications and Strategies for Traders,* R. Fischer (New York: Wiley, 1993), p. 60.

Stop-Loss Rules

Whenever a market position is entered, one must protect it with a stop-loss or stop-reverse signal.

When analyzing and dealing with corrections, our opinion is that the best stop-loss protection should be below the starting point of the first impulse wave (Figure 3.4).

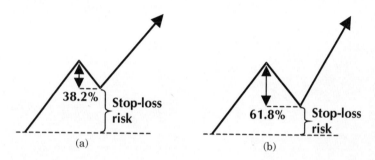

Figure 3.4 Different stop-loss risk profiles on investments into (a) a correction of 38.2% and (b) a correction of 61.8%. *Source:* FAM Research, 2000.

This stop level is our preference. Most of the time, stop-loss levels are selected as a point value or a dollar value, which is then placed below the entry price (for buy signals; the rule works in reverse for sell signals).

Question 3–3:
What is the logic behind our strategy of placing the stop level below the starting point of the previous impulse wave instead of working with a stop-loss based on a dollar value or basis point?

Profit Target Rules

Profit targets, for use with corrections, are created by directly applying the key ratios—0.618, 1.000, and 1.618—from the Fibonacci summation series.

For the calculation of profit targets, we take the total amplitude of the first impulse wave of a market move upward or downward and multiply it by one of the aforementioned Fibonacci ratios (Figure 3.5).

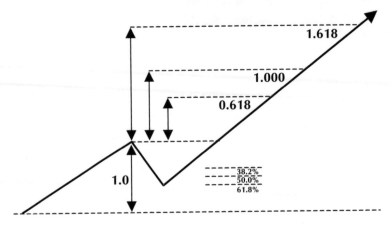

Figure 3.5 Alternative levels of corrections in combination with different ratios of profit targets. *Source:* FAM Research, 2000.

Question 3–4:
Why might working with fixed profit-target rules be such an important element in a short-term-oriented investment strategy?

Trailing Stop Rules

To better protect accumulated profits in an open market position, we recommend applying a trailing stop in addition to working with a profit target.

The trailing stop is not always the best solution, but it does protect at least some of the profits after the market has moved in a profitable direction. On the other hand, one might get stopped out with a small profit before the market starts another strong rise, which will then be missed.

Depending on the product and its volatility, a three- to four-day trailing stop is always helpful.

Figure 3.6 is an illustration of a trailing stop set to a four-day low on a long position.

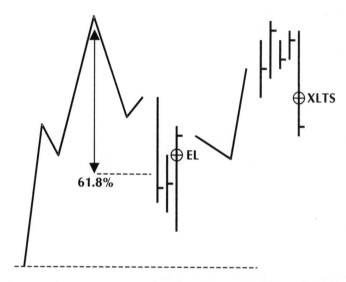

Figure 3.6   Profit protection using a trailing stop. *Source:* **FAM Research, 2000.**

Re-entry Rules

After a position is stopped out in a loss and the market price moves back to its original direction, one often questions whether it should be followed by a re-entry signal.

Working with corrections means one must always invest in the direction of the main trend.

When we work with a sensitive main-entry rule, there is always the probability of getting stopped out when buying at a previous day's high after a 61.8% correction. If we suffer a stop-loss out of a long position (vice versa for a stop-loss out of a short position), we recommend a re-entry buy signal at the previous four days' high.

Question 3–5:

In Figure 3.7, why do we use two different entry rules for the original market entry long and the re-entry?

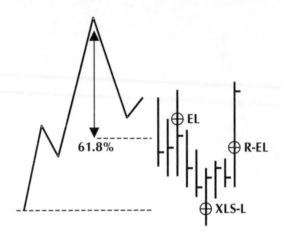

Figure 3.7   Four days' high re-entry after stop-loss. *Source:* FAM Research, 2000.

Linear versus Semilogarithmic Scales

Elliott and his followers could never agree on whether the analysis of chart patterns should be done using a linear scale or a semilogarithmic scale, or both.

A correction in price of 38.2% on an impulse wave of 1,000 ticks remains 382 ticks, no matter what chart scaling is applied.

What we are presenting here is an approach in which corrections are not measured in points, but are graphically and geometrically calculated by measuring distances from swing highs to swing lows in centimeters or equivalents.

In the pair of charts shown in Figure 3.8, we compare a weekly price move in the S&P500 Index between June 1996 and December 2000 on a linear chart (a) and a semilogarithmic chart (b).

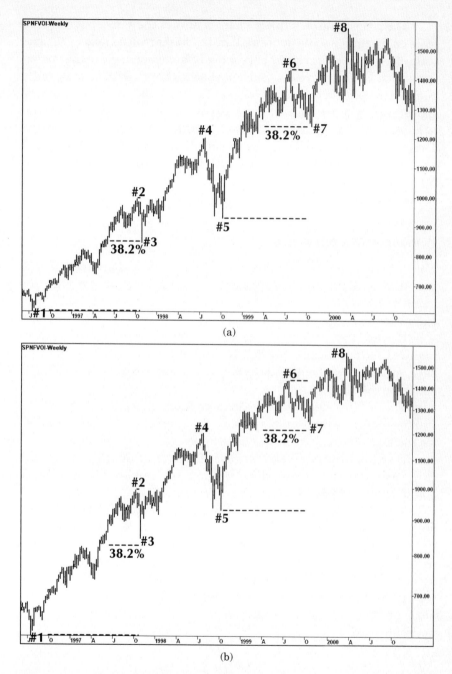

Figure 3.8   Weekly S&P500 Index from 06–96 to 12–00. (a) Linear versus (b) semilogarithmic scaling. *Source:* FAM Research, 2000.

The price scale on a linear chart is always the same, but the price scale on a semilog scale gets smaller, the higher we go up on the price scale. These differences can have a big effect when measuring corrections with Fibonacci ratios. Such deviations occur with semilogarithmic charts because their starting points determine the final graphical appearance of a price move. The starting point of a semilog scale has to be chosen subjectively, regardless of whether we want to measure distances in price (vertically) or in time (horizontally).

As Elliott pointed out, working with semilog scales can be helpful as an additional means of analysis when applied to linear scaling at the same time.

Working with Corrections

Working with corrections takes a lot of discipline and accuracy. Profit potential is highest in very volatile products, such as the S&P500 Index and the DAX30 Index, or in cash currencies and volatile individual stocks.

However, volatility is not enough; volatility *and* high volume are required for successful trading. If liquidity is insufficient, the slippage getting in and out of the position becomes so big that trading is not recommended.

The biggest decision any investor must make before he or she starts trading is the swing size and the correction to be calculated, for the size of a market swing determines whether a market move is considered big or small, slow or fast. There is no simple and perfect rule. In our analysis, we work with a minimum swing size of 80 basis points in the S&P500 Index (a move from 1,400.00 to 1,480.00).

Another major problem is distinguishing when a market is in an uptrend, or when a trend has turned to the downside. If market prices are forming new lows and the swing size from the previous peak is more than the minimum swing size, we will have a sell signal as soon as our precalculated correction level (e.g., 61.8%) is reached. But we will never know whether we are selling into a correction of a previous impulse wave in a downtrend or into the impulse wave of a new uptrend.

This is why working with a higher correction level and a bigger swing size is recommended. Although we might calculate the direction of the impulse wave incorrectly, the risk remains low, and we still have a chance of getting out of the position without too much damage (Figure 3.9).

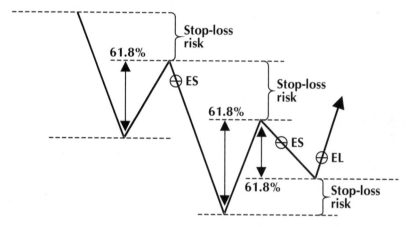

Figure 3.9 Risk levels if a correction is already the impulse wave of a new trend movement. *Source:* FAM Research, 2000.

Taking the S&P500 Index as a trading example, we use the following parameters:

- Correction level of 61.8%; swing size of 80 basis points;

- Profit target level set to 0.618 times the total swing size of the previous impulse wave; trailing stop level set to four days' high after market entry on sells (or four days' low on buys); stop-loss level set at the low of the first impulse wave (for buy signals; vice versa for sell signals);

- No re-entry rule.

Exercise 3–B:

To practice the calculation of corrections, complete the following tasks:

(a) **On the S&P500 Index daily bar chart (Figure 3.10), identify the significant peaks and valleys and then mark the corrections that reach the 61.8% correction level.**

(b) **When the corrections are marked, identify the entry signals and exit signals, based on the given parameters, and mark them on the chart.**

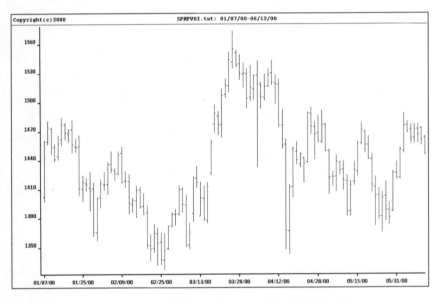

Figure 3.10 S&P500 Index from 01–00 to 06–00.

Taking the Japanese Yen cash currency as a second trading example, we use the following parameters:

- Correction level of 61.8%;

- Swing size of 1.80 JPY (e.g., a move from 110.00 to 111.80);

- Entry rule at previous day's high or low; no re-entry rule;

- Profit target level set to 0.618 times the total swing size of the previous impulse wave; trailing stop level set to four days' high after market entry on sells (or four days' low on buys); stop-loss level set at the low of the first impulse wave (for buy signals; vice versa for sell signals).

Exercise 3–C:
To practice the calculation of corrections, complete the following tasks:

(a) **On the Japanese Yen cash currency daily bar chart (Figure 3.11), mark the significant highs and lows and the 61.8% correction levels.**

(b) **When the correction levels are marked, show the buy and sell signals based on the given parameters.**

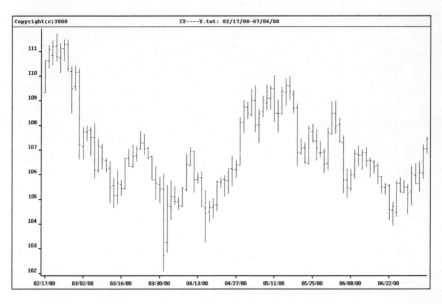

Figure 3.11   Japanese Yen cash currency from 02–00 to 07–00.

Corrections on a Weekly Basis

Working with weekly data means that we expect some bigger trend changes, which we can exploit by trading corrections.

Long-term traders are looking for big swings. However, even in long-term trading products, there are times when products like the S&P500 Index or the Japanese Yen cash currency are not trending at all. The year 2000 offered a good example of these liquid products trading in a narrow price range.

Working with weekly data based on correction levels is problematic, for one never knows whether markets are in a trending state or in a sideward condition. Compared with our analysis on daily data, we find exaggeration on a weekly basis where trading approaches can either be extremely good or very bad.

Big market moves can be caught when the size of a correction is calculated correctly, but if we choose the wrong retracement level, we either miss major moves completely, or suffer losses bigger than those we would experience on a daily basis. This happens because we cannot stay as close to the markets when we have weekly data instead of daily data. Swings from one week to another are larger than day-to-day swings, so stop-loss levels, trailing stops, or profit targets might (pointwise) be far away from the entry levels.

The following example, based on the S&P500 Index, illustrates what can happen to an approach based on corrections in a weekly sideward market that lasts over a longer period of time. We will work with the following parameters:

- Retracement level of 38.2%; minimum swing size of 140 basis points (e.g., a move from 1,400.00 to 1,540.00 from valley to peak);

- Profit target level set to 0.618 times the total swing size of the previous impulse wave; trailing stop level set to two weeks' high after market entry on sells (or four days' low on buys); stop-loss level set to previous week's low (for buy signals; vice versa for sell signals).

Exercise 3–D:

Complete the following steps on the weekly S&P500 Index chart in Figure 3.12:

(a) **Mark the significant peaks and valleys based on a minimum swing size of 140 basis points and corresponding retracement levels of 38.2%.**

(b) **Mark the entry and exit points based on the entry rule, the stop-loss protection, and the trailing stop rule, as mentioned in the parameters above.**

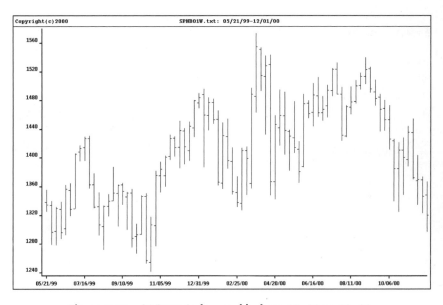

Figure 3.12   S&P500 Index weekly from 05–99 to 12–00.

The corrections described in this chapter have principally affected daily and weekly data.

We will now proceed to the description and analysis of extensions. Extensions can be turned into very useful Fibonacci-related trading tools and can work just as effectively as corrections on a daily basis.

EXTENSIONS

Extensions are exuberant price movements that result from runaway markets, opening gaps, or limit-up/limit-down moves at high volatility.

Extensions usually occur when traders receive unexpected news concerning weather conditions, crop reports, or interest rate changes. The reactions to such news are often powerful enough to reverse trend directions.

To explain the characteristics of extensions theoretically, we return to Elliott's wave principles. Elliott observed correctly that extensions can often be expected in the 3-wave pattern or in the second impulse wave of any price move.

Extensions in 3-Wave Patterns

In a regular 3-wave pattern in an uptrend, the correction does not go lower than the bottom of wave 1, whereas in extensions out of bull-trap or bear-trap formations (irregular tops or bottoms), the corrections can go higher than the high of the first impulse wave, or lower than the low of the first impulse wave, respectively.

Figure 3.13 illustrates two different cases of extensions out of regular and irregular chart formations.

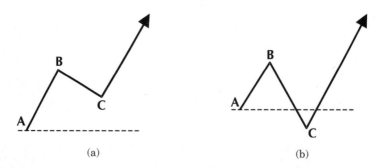

(a)   (b)

Figure 3.13   Extensions out of (a) a regular 3-wave pattern and (b) a bear-trap chart formation. *Source:* FAM Research, 2000.

Working with extensions means trading against major trend directions. It also suggests that an investor is looking for quick profits by taking advantage of imbalances in the marketplace. Therefore, it is important to know not only when to enter a position in advance, but also when to exit a position.

Three consecutive steps must be taken when calculating price targets in extensions of the third wave out of a 3-wave chart formation:

1. A minimum swing size must be defined as the size from peak to valley, or valley to peak, of the first impulse wave of the 3-wave pattern.

2. The swing size must be multiplied by the Fibonacci ratio 1.618.

3. The resulting value must be added to the size of the initiating swing to define the price target.

Exercise 3–E:

In the following 3-wave pattern, the first impulse wave is measured 1.0 from valley A to peak B. Complete the chart in Figure 3.14 by calculating the price target at a peak D, using the Fibonacci ratio 1.618.

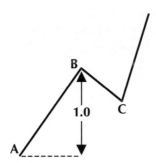

Figure 3.14   Extension in the third wave of a 3-wave pattern uptrend. Target price level measured by the Fibonacci ration PHI = 1.618.

When extensions were introduced as geometric Fibonacci trading tools in the first chapter, we described alternative ratios of the Fibonacci summation series as valid measurements for the size of extensions. This general statement still holds true. However, to explain the use of extensions, we limit our analysis to PHI as the Fibonacci ratio 1.618, for this is the most commonly used ratio when working with extensions.

Question 3–6:
Based on what has been explained so far in this chapter, what do you think is the most important variable in the analysis of extensions?

Working with Fibonacci price targets in extensions leads to three different scenarios. Market prices can (a) come close to the precalculated price, but miss it by a small margin; (b) reach the exact target price; or (c) overshoot the target price.

In real-time trading, this means that if, for example, we have a price target in the S&P500 Index at 1,300.00 and the market price is trading at 1,250.00, the upper price band would be 1% above (1,313.00) and the lower price band would be 1% below (1,287.00). This 1% level is a good estimate, but it could change with the swing size or the volatility of a product.

In addition to the size of the impulse swing, a few other parameters (entry rules, stop-loss rules, and profit target rules) determine the successful application of extensions. These are explained in the following sections.

Entry Rules

By integrating an entry rule, a countertrend investment strategy can be fine-tuned.

As explained above, we have to differentiate three possible scenarios when considering the price band. An entry rule is necessary to make the early stage of a market position more flexible and reliable.

The application of an entry rule leads to a slightly reduced profit potential, because positions are entered with a time lag after the target price has been reached. Trades become safer, however, because positions are protected from excessive losses in cases where strongly rising or falling market prices do not stop at the precalculated price targets.

Exercise 3–F:
We will work with two different entry rules: (a) in an uptrend we sell after the price target is reached and a two-day low is broken, or (b) as a "market on close" order, if the close of a trading day is lower than the close of the highest day within the price band.

Complete the two charts in Figure 3.15 according to entry rules (a) and (b).

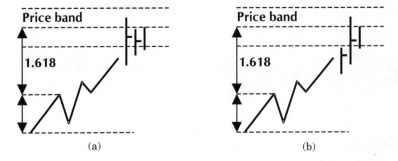

Figure 3.15   Entry rules out of a price band. *Source:* FAM Research, 2000.

Stop-Loss Rules

Whenever a market position is established long or short, it has to be protected with a stop-loss.

The rule for short positions is that the stop-loss protection is placed one tick above the highest swing high after the short signal has been received. For buy signals, the stop-loss is placed one tick below the lowest swing low after the long signal has been received. Figure 3.16 illustrates the stop-loss rule for a short position.

Figure 3.16   Stop-loss proteaction on a short position. *Source:* FAM Research, 2000.

Profit Target Rules and Trailing Stop Rules

Profit targets are useful for working with volatile market swings. The limit order is placed before the profit target is reached. The smaller the initial swing size chosen, the closer the entry level and profit target level. This is one reason to work with an initial swing size that is not too small; otherwise, there is not enough profit potential for a trade.

We consider a profit target of 50% of the total initial move a reasonable goal. The profit target level for a short position is defined as 50% of the total distance from the swing low of the first impulse wave, up to the price target line of the extension (vice versa for a long position). Whenever the market moves toward a 50% profit target, we have the option to take the profit at the 50% level, or to work with a trailing stop rule instead. If a trailing stop rule is preferred, we recommend a previous four days' high or low as the exit rule.

In comparison with a general 50% profit target rule, profits can be greater or slightly smaller, based on a trailing stop rule. In addition, trailing stop rules can realize small profits even in cases where the 50% profit target level is not reached. Figure 3.17 shows all three exit options.

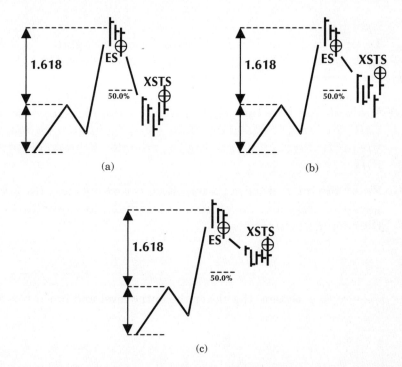

Figure 3.17   Trailing stop configurations. (a) Increased profit potential; (b) re-duced profit potential; (c) profit potential (profit target not reached). *Source: FAM Research, 2000.*

Working with Extensions

In this section, we show two examples of how to apply the rules for extensions to daily price charts. The Japanese Yen cash currency, the first example, has the following parameters:

- Minimum swing size of 1.80 JPY (e.g., a move from 110.00 to 111.80 from valley to peak);

- Price target of the extension in PHI distance 1.618 times the swing size of the first impulse wave;

- Profit target level set to 50% of the total distance from the bottom or top of the impulse wave to the price target; stop-loss level set to the highest high before entry on sells and the lowest low before entry on buys.

Exercise 3–G:

To practice working with extensions, complete the following exercises on the chart of the daily Japanese Yen cash currency price data (Figure 3.18):

(a) **Mark all price swings that have a minimum swing size of 1.80 JPY, and, if based on these significant swings, mark the profit target levels using the common Fibonacci ratio PHI = 1.618.**

(b) **Enter the buy/sell signals based on the entry rule, the 50% profit target rule, and the stop-loss rule, as described in the above parameters.**

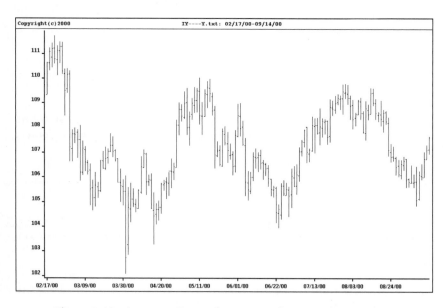

Figure 3.18   Japanese Yen cash currency from 02–00 to 09–00.

Signals similar to the ones defined for the Japanese Yen cash currency can be generated for the DAX30 Index, using the following parameters:

- Minimum swing size of 400 points (e.g., a move from 6,500.0 to 6,900.0 from valley to peak);

- Price target of the extension in PHI distance 1.618 times the swing size of the first impulse wave;

- Trailing stop level set to four days' high on sell signals and four days' low on buy signals;

- Stop-loss level set to the highest high before entry on sells and the lowest low before entry on buys;

- Re-entry rule after a stop-loss on closes below the price target line for sell signals and on closes above the price target line for buy signals.

Exercise 3–H:

To practice working with extensions, complete the following exercises on the chart of daily DAX30 Index price data (Figure 3.19):

- **(a) Mark all price swings that have a minimum swing size of 400 basis points.**

- **(b) Based on these significant swing highs and swing lows, mark the profit target levels using the common Fibonacci ratio PHI = 1.618.**

- **(c) Enter the buy/sell signals based on entry rule, 50% profit target rule, and stop-loss rule, as described in the above parameters.**

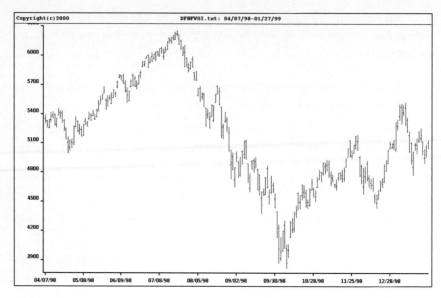

Figure 3.19   DAX30 Index from 04–98 to 01–99.

Extensions in 5-Wave Patterns

When analyzing extensions in 5-wave patterns, we look for an additional parameter, based on the Fibonacci summation series, that will confirm our price target calculation for extensions out of a 3-wave pattern.

To analyze a 3-wave pattern, we multiply the size of the first impulse wave by the Fibonacci ratio 1.618. This number is then added to the swing size of the initial move to calculate a Fibonacci price target. We expect this line to be the end of the third wave; it should result in a correction once the market price reaches this price level.

We usually have more than three waves in a trending market, so our approach to calculating a Fibonacci target price must be slightly modified. The most common market price pattern has at least five waves; three are impulse waves and two are corrective waves.

In a regular 5-wave move in an uptrend, the price target line for the end of wave 5 is calculated by multiplying the amplitude of wave

1 by the Fibonacci ratio 1.618, and then multiplying the amplitude from the bottom of wave 1 to the top of wave 3 by the ratio's reciprocal value 0.618.

By combining the two calculations—Fibonacci ratios 0.618 and 1.618—we can precalculate the end of wave 5 exactly at the same price level, given that the market moves in a regular price pattern (Figure 3.20).

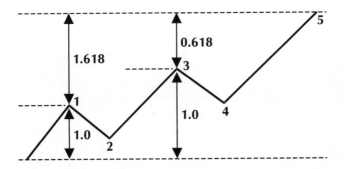

Figure 3.20 Calculation of Fibonacci price target in a regular 5-wave move. *Source:* FAM Research, 2000.

In reality, regular market price movements occur very infrequently. Applying Elliott's wave principles to market prices is idealistic because, almost always, we are dealing with irregular price moves.

Price Bands

What makes a 5-wave pattern so interesting is that the integration of 5-wave moves into our analysis allows us to calculate Fibonacci price-target bands, which give investors a very good indication of what price targets to use.

As long as the upper end and the lower end of a price band are close together, we can use them as valid price indicators for the targets of extensions.

Exercise 3–I:

In Figure 3.21, we show a weekly bar chart of the DAX30 Index from January 2000 to December 2000. Significant turning points in the market are designated #1, #2, #3, and #4.

Answer questions (a) and (b) and use the resultant figures to complete task (c):

(a) The distance from #1 to #2 is the first wave and should be multiplied by which Fibonacci ratio?

(b) The distance from #1 to #4 is the third wave and should be multiplied by which Fibonacci ratio?

(c) Integrate both calculations into the chart in Figure 3.21, and mark the time band that results.

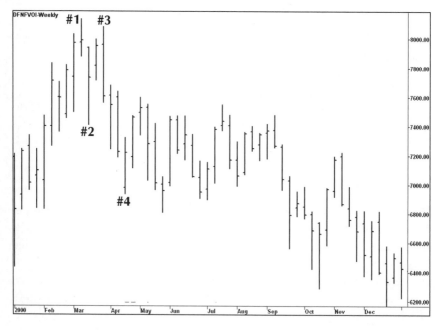

Figure 3.21   DAX30 Index from 01–00 to 12–00.

5-Wave Patterns and the Fibonacci Summation Series

In the previous section, we pointed out how important it is for the quality of a price target to be confirmed by different waves, and to be precalculated by making use of more than one of the Fibonacci-related ratios.

The more confirmations we can generate from a potential turning point, the better our trading decision. To get more information from the price target band, we integrate the figures of the Fibonacci summation series into the weekly chart of the DAX30 Index data.

Figure 3.22 shows the price band of the 3-wave and 5-wave extensions in combination with the time targets calculated using the Fibonacci summation series.

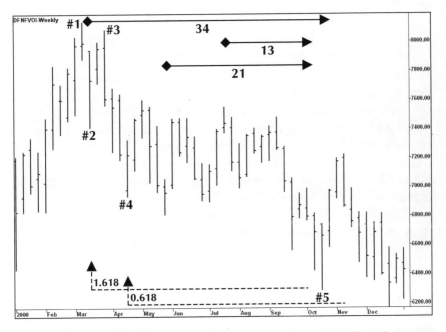

Figure 3.22   Chart of the DAX30 Index from 01–00 to 12–00. The price target corridor and Fibonacci summation series are combined. (Disclaimer: Past performance may not be indicative of future results.) *Source:* **FAM Research, 2000.**

The results of our calculation are stunning:

- A total of 33 weeks separates the week with the highest day (8,136.0 in March 2000) from the week with the lowest day (6,340.0 in October 2000). The number 34 (part of Fibonacci's summation series) is reached one week after the lowest low is made.

- There are 21 weeks, beginning with the major valley at 6,811.0 in May 2000 and counting up to exactly one week before the lowest low, 6,340.0, is made in October 2000.

- There are 13 weeks from the major peak at 7,550.0 in July 2000 up to exactly one week before the lowest low is reached in October 2000, at 6,340.0.

ANSWERS TO QUESTIONS AND EXERCISES

In this chapter, we introduced corrections and extensions as geometric Fibonacci trading devices.

Although we show how to properly work with them, it is still a small portion of what is covered in the textbook, where each example can be reproduced with the WINPHI program and its historical data. The answers to the questions and exercises in this chapter are explained in more detail on pages 53–79 (on corrections) and 79–104 (on extensions) in *The New Fibonacci Trader*.

By the time this book is read, there will be a significant time gap of at least several months. Interested readers should, therefore, go to an online version of the WINPHI software package that we have set up at **www.fibotrader.com** on a registered membership basis.

Exercise 3–A:

The shorter the time compression, the bigger the problem with false breakouts. One of the reasons for this is that floor traders often buy at new lows and sell at new highs.

The correct completion of the two graphs follows the scheme in Figure 3.23.

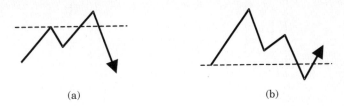

(a)   (b)

Figure 3.23   (a) False breakout to the upside; (b) false breakout to the down-side. *Source:* FAM Research, 2000.

Answer to Question 3–1:

Some of the conditions affecting safe investment in corrections include:

- Consistency in the investment strategy;

- The volatility of a product (which can vary greatly among cash currencies, commodities, futures, single stocks, or mutual funds);

- The size of the original swing size on which a retracement is measured;

- The strength of a trend;

- The data compression rate (whether we work with weekly, daily, or intraday data).

Answer to Question 3–2:

We suggest that the close of each of the five trading days will equal the high on a "plus day" and the low on a "minus day." If we work with a filter that eliminates all movements smaller than 50 ticks, the two days within the correction with the price bars each of which has 20 ticks, are eliminated, because the correction of a total of 40 ticks is smaller than the filter of 50 ticks. Working with filters helps to eliminate noise in price swings, especially on intraday data and volatile markets (Figure 3.24).

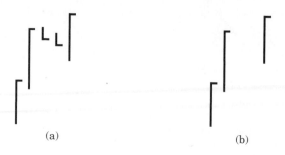

(a)

(b)

Figure 3.24 Sample market move of five days (a) without filter and (b) with filter. *Source:* **FAM Research, 2000.**

Answer to Question 3–3:

If we stay within the framework of the Elliott wave principles, we usually have a 3-wave pattern, out of which wave 1 and wave 3 are impulse waves, and wave 2 is a correction.

This concept is, in our opinion, one of Elliott's biggest discoveries. We can only consider wave 3 an impulse wave if wave 2 does not go lower than the beginning of the first impulse wave. If it goes below the beginning of the first impulse wave, it is likely that the entire trend has changed and has not just been corrected. In this case, we can no longer expect the next impulse wave to be in favor of our current trading signal.

Setting the stop-loss protection to the low of the first impulse wave also means that the earlier we invest in the correction, the farther the stop-loss point is going to be from the current market price. If we wait for a larger correction, we have a much closer stop-loss protection, but we run the risk of missing a price move.

Answer to Question 3–4:

In real-time trading, the market does not always act in our favor, regardless of the profit target we choose. If the profit target is reached at 0.618 times the strength of the previous impulse wave, the market price might move higher, but if we place the profit target at 1.618 times the amplitude of the previous impulse wave, the market price might not reach this level.

What is important is *consistency* in creating and following trading signals. This is where computerized test runs become very important. If we compare the profitability of the respective profit targets on historical data with what is supplied by computer programs, we find that we are not always correct. However, this encourages us to act within a framework that will provide us with the best average profit potential available.

Answer to Question 3–5:

The more conservative re-entry rule, in comparison with the main entry rule, is necessary to confirm a trend reversal. The re-entry rule makes sense if we begin working with a very tight entry rule and a very close stop-loss protection. Using such a strategy, we limit the risk in a position. By applying a 61.8% correction level, we get very close to the bottom of the previous impulse wave and reduce risk to a reasonable size.

Exercise 3–B:

Seven sample signals for the S&P500 Index between January and June 2000 are tabulated for their entry rule, exit rule, and profit/loss ratio. (See Table 3.2.)

Table 3.2   Seven Sample Signals

High#/Low# Reference	Entry Rule		Exit Rule		Profit/ (Loss) in Points
H#1/L#2	Entry sell	1,427.50	Stop-loss	1,449.80	(22.30)
H#3/L#4	Entry sell	1,386.20	Rev. buy	1,385.50	0.70
L#4/H#5	Rev. buy	1,385.50	Profit target	1,477.90	92.40
H#5a/L#6	Entry sell	1,517.50	Profit target	1,351.30	166.20
H#7/L#8	Entry sell	1,467.00	Rev. buy	1,419.00	48.00
L#8/H#9	Rev. buy	1,419.00	Rev. sell	1,456.00	37.00
H#9/L#10	Rev. sell	1,456.00	Trail. stop	1,418.00	38.00

In Figure 3.25, the seven S&P500 Index sample trading signals have been applied to the chart. We find the respective time period in 2000 interesting for demonstration purposes because it includes all combinations of the signals we described earlier (although this does not mean that these signals will repeat themselves in the future or are an indication of future results).

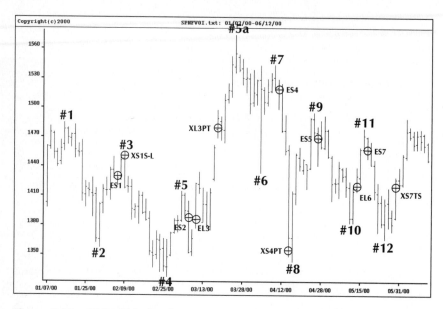

Figure 3.25   S&P500 Index from 01–00 to 06–00. (Disclaimer: Past performance may not be indicative of future results.)

Exercise 3–C:

Six sample signals for the Japanese Yen cash currency can be generated between January and September 2000. This time span includes all of the trading signals we have described in the course of this chapter. However, the time span is too short to be representative of future trading results.

It is important to understand that these results are not computer-tested. We have chosen the products and parameters only to give the reader ideas and to demonstrate new, profitable, money-making strategies.

The performance profile for the six trading signals, including their entry rule, exit rule, and profit/loss ratio, is shown in Table 3.3.

Table 3.3   Six Trading Signals

High#/Low# Reference	Entry Rule		Exit Rule		Profit/ (Loss) in Points
L#2/H#3	Entry buy	105.90	Stop-loss	104.65	(1.25)
H#3/L#4	Entry sell	106.35	Rev. buy	104.95	1.40
L#4/H#5	Rev. buy	104.95	Trail. stop	107.71	2.76
L#8/H#9	Entry buy	109.04	Rev. sell	109.05	0.01
H#9/L#10	Rev. sell	109.05	Trail. stop	107.91	1.14
H#11/L#12	Entry sell	107.67	Rev. buy	105.63	2.04

Figure 3.26 shows the six Japanese Yen cash currency sample trading signals applied to the chart.

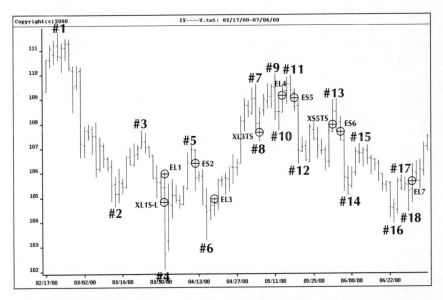

Figure 3.26   Japanese Yen cash currency from 02–00 to 07–00. (Disclaimer: Past performance may not be indicative of future results.)

Exercise 3–D:

The performance profile for six sample trading signals in the weekly S&P500 Index, including their entry rule, exit rule, and profit/loss ratio, is shown in Table 3.4.

Table 3.4 Six Sample Trading Signals

High#/Low# Reference	Entry Rule		Exit Rule		Profit/ (Loss) in Points
H#1/L#2	Entry sell	1,340.40	Trail. stop	1,348.00	(7.60)
L#2a/H#3	Entry buy	1,449.80	Stop-loss	1,357.00	(92.80)
L#4/H#5	Entry buy	1,459.50	Rev. sell	1,417.00	(42.50)
H#5/L#6	Rev. sell	1,417.00	Rev. buy	1,439.50	(22.50)
L#6/H#7	Rev. buy	1,439.50	Stop-loss	1,382.50	(57.50)
H#7a/L#8	Entry sell	1,388.50	Still open	1,337.70	40.80

In Figure 3.27, we show the six signals applied to the chart.

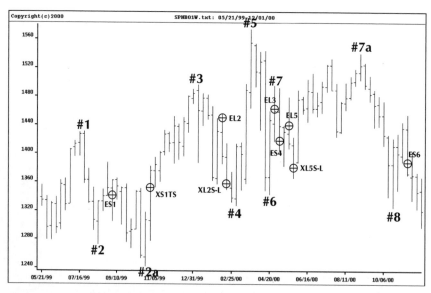

Figure 3.27   S&P500 Index weekly from 05–99 to 12–00. (Disclaimer: Past performance may not be indicative of future results.)

Figure 3.27, which shows the S&P500 Index weekly data from May 1999 to December 2000, illustrates what can happen to an approach based on corrections if we use weekly data and if the sideward market lasts over a longer period of time.

This book is meant to be an educational tool. Therefore, it is important to present bad scenarios that can occur, even with the best looking trading strategy as well as successful ones.

Considering the advantages and disadvantages of corrections on a weekly basis, we do not recommend the application of corrections as a means of analyzing weekly data.

Exercise 3–E:

The swing size—from peak to valley, or valley to peak—of the initial impulse wave is set as 1.0, which is the basis for determining the target price.

The graph to define the target price at peak D, based on the calculation of an extension using the Fibonacci ratio PHI = 1.618, must be completed according to Figure 3.28.

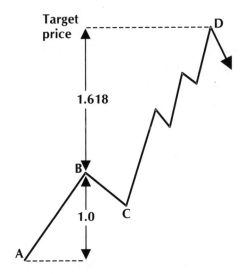

Figure 3.28 Extension in the third wave of a 3-wave pattern uptrend. Target price level measured by the Fibonacci ratio PHI = 1.618. *Source:* FAM Research, 2000.

Answer to Question 3–6:

The most important variable in the analysis with extensions is the swing size. If the swing size is too small, the thrust of the extension might be too big and may overshoot the precalculated price target by a wide margin; but if the swing size is too big, it might take weeks or months to reach a price target.

Exercise 3–F:

The completion of the two graphs according to entry rules (a) and (b) must match Figure 3.29.

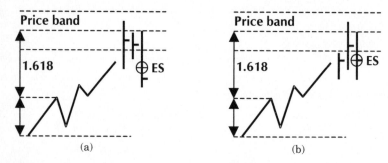

(a)　　　　　(b)

Figure 3.29   Entry rules out of a price band at the target price line of an extension; (a) entry on previous two days' low; (b) entry on close before highest day's close. *Source:* FAM Research, 2000.

Exercise 3–G:

The performance profile for four sample trading signals in the Japanese Yen cash currency is shown in Table 3.5.

Table 3.5   Four Sample Trading Signals

High#/Low# Reference	Entry Rule		Exit Rule		Profit/ (Loss) in Points
H#1/L#2	Entry buy	105.50	Profit target	107.60	2.10
H#3/L#4	Entry buy	105.65	Profit target	107.10	1.45
L#5/H#6	Entry sell	108.53	Stop-loss	109.38	(0.85)
H#7/L#8	Entry buy	106.45	Profit target	107.32	0.87

Figure 3.30 shows the entry and exit signals for the Japanese Yen cash currency from February to August 2000. This period is interesting for demonstration purposes because it has three signals where profit-target levels are triggered.

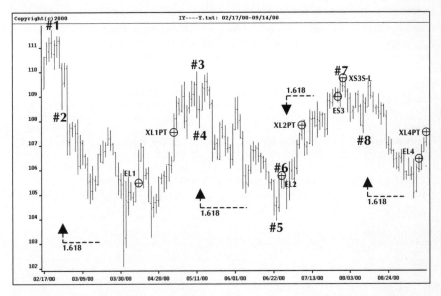

Figure 3.30 Japanese Yen cash currency from 02–00 to 09–00. (Disclaimer: Past performance may not be indicative of future results.)

Exercise 3–H:

Buy and sell signals for the DAX30 Index from April 1998 to January 1999 are shown in Figure 3.31. We chose this period because it is a good representation of signals with extensions based on the parameters for these signals. Four signals are shown where profit targets are triggered and entry signals and exit signals are executed according to the appropriate rules.

Tables 3.6 and 3.7 show the performance profiles of triggered entry and exit signals with corresponding entry and exit prices. Calculations on all four sample signals in the DAX30 Index have been separately conducted for profit-target exits and for trailing stop exits.

Table 3.6 Profit Target Exits

High#/Low# Reference	Entry Rule		Exit Rule		Profit/ (Loss) in Points
L#1/H#2	Sell	6,005.0	Profit target	5,545.5	449.5
H#3/L#4	Entry buy	4,204.0	Stop-loss	3,861.0	(143.0)
H#3/L#4	Rebuy	4,299.0	Profit target	4,961.0	662.0
L#6/H#7	Entry sell	4,960.0	Stop-loss	5,189.5	(229.5)

Table 3.7 Trailing Stop Exits

High#/Low# Reference	Entry Rule		Exit Rule		Profit/ (Loss) in Points
L#1/H#2	Sell	6,005.0	Trail. stop	5,520.0	485.0
H#3/L#4	Entry buy	4,204.0	Stop-loss	3,861.0	(143.0)
H#3/L#4	Rebuy	4,299.0	Trail. stop	4,960.0	661.0
L#6/H#7	Entry sell	4,960.0	Trail. stop	4,720.0	240.0

Figure 3.31 DAX30 Index from 04–98 to 02–99. (Disclaimer: Past performance may not be indicative of future results.)

Exercise 3–I:

The swing size of the first impulse move, from the high in the DAX30 Index chart at 8,136.0 to the low at 7,412.0, and multiplied by the Fibonacci ratio 1.618, leads us to the upper end of the price band of 6,305.0.

The lower end of the price band is calculated with the third wave from the high of wave 1 at 8,136.0 to the low of wave 3 (peak #3 to valley #4) at 6,937.0, multiplied by 0.618 and resulting in 6,197.0.

The result of the calculations with the Fibonacci ratios (1.618 for the first wave and 0.618 for the third wave) is the price band, which is the distance from 6,305.0 to 6,197.0. This is less than the setting of 200 points, which is the maximum size we consider reasonable while applying this strategy to the DAX30 Index.

Figure 3.32 shows the price band out of a 5-wave pattern.

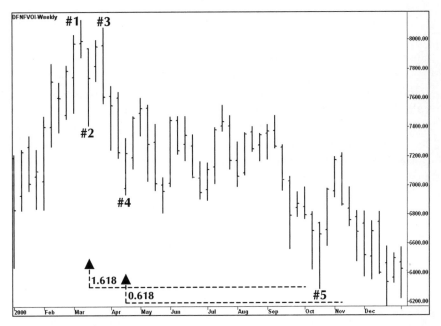

Figure 3.32   DAX30 Index from 01–00 to 12–00. (Disclaimer: Past performance may not be indicative of future results.)

FINAL REMARKS

In the first major section of this chapter, corrections as Fibonacci trading tools were discussed in principle. Three correction levels—38.2%, 50.0%, and 61.8%—are directly derived from the Fibonacci summation series. In volatile products such as the S&P500 Index, the Japanese Yen cash currency, or the DAX30 Index, we recommend working with the correction level of 61.8%.

However, the swing size of the first impulse wave (from which we measure the correction) is just as important as the correction level itself. The larger the swing size, the better the chances for a profitable investment as soon as the 61.8% retracement level is reached. Also, the larger the swing size, the more sensitive the entry rules for any investment (e.g., the previous high versus a previous four days' high).

Extensions are then discussed, first out of 3-wave patterns, then out of 5-wave patterns, and finally out of 5-wave patterns in combination with the counts of the Fibonacci summation series.

Time and price targets do not always come together on the same day or the same week, but this is not important. What is important is the combination of price bands and time bands.

In contrast to technical analysis, where market movements are followed with a time lag, working with Fibonacci devices aims at calculating major highs or lows in advance. If applied properly, the Fibonacci trading tools are able to forecast with an accuracy that few other investment tools can match, as long as the investor has the patience to wait, the strength to believe in the power of the Fibonacci tools, and the discipline to invest once target prices are reached.

4

PHI-Channels

Human behavior is reflected in chart patterns as large swings, small swings, trend formations, and sideward markets. Human behavior is also expressed in peak and valley formations.

By introducing PHI-channels, or Fibonacci trend channels, as independent Fibonacci trading tools, we make use of peak and valley formations in the markets, which helps us to safely forecast major changes in trend directions.

We will start this chapter with a brief description of the general structure of regular trend channels, and then discuss PHI-channels as specific types of trend channels. We will also present examples of how to successfully work with PHI-channels as indicators for market trend changes.

STRUCTURE OF REGULAR TREND CHANNELS

Regular trend channels are graphically generated by drawing parallel lines through peaks and valleys of market price moves. Every peak and/or valley in the markets serves as a prominent indication of what the majority of investors think at any particular moment in time.

The significance of peaks and valleys becomes more evident with the particular data compression analyzed.

Intraday peaks or valleys are less meaningful indicators than the peaks or valleys tracked on a daily basis, but the daily peaks or valleys are not as revealing as the peaks or valleys on weekly charts. Therefore, to demonstrate how powerful trend channels can be as investment tools, we will concentrate on daily and weekly charts.

In contrast to the corrections and extensions in the previous chapter, we do not use PHI-channels to generate trading signals. Instead, we strengthen the overall Fibonacci analysis by applying trend channels as indicators for trend changes. Such indicators serve as additional confirmations of trading signals generated by one of the other Fibonacci trading tools.

Peak and valley formations in general trading are of much greater significance than traders may realize. It is important to analyze peaks and valleys, not only as stand-alone patterns of trend reversals, but also for the ways in which peaks and valleys are related to each other (Figure 4.1).

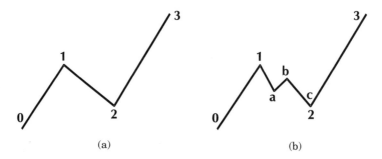

Figure 4.1   (a) Regular correction in an uptrend; (b) irregular correction in an uptrend. *Source:* **FAM Research, 2000.**

In an uptrend, the peak at point #3 will be higher than the preceding peak at point #1 (if the correction from point #1 to point #2 is regular). An irregular correction in an uptrend results in a peak that is lower than the preceding peak. In this case, we have an a-b-c correction; the peak at point b is lower than the corresponding peak at point #1.

The basic graphical scheme for creating regular trend channels using 3-wave moves in uptrends or downtrends is illustrated in Figure 4.2.

In regular 3-wave price moves, we can connect the bottom of the first impulse wave at point #0 with the bottom of the correction at point #2, and then draw a parallel through the top of the first peak at point #1. The resulting line will be considered an indication of an upcoming peak of wave #3 as soon as wave #3 touches the line.

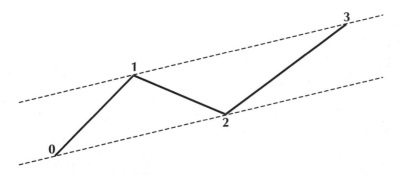

Figure 4.2   Regular trend channel in an uptrend. *Source:* FAM Research, 2000.

In a regular 5-wave price pattern, the bottom of wave #4 is expected to touch the extension line drawn from point #0 through point #2. The corresponding peak at the end of the wave lies on the parallel line that marks the upper border of the trend channel. Wave #5, in this respect, is the third impulse wave of a regular 5-wave move.

Following Elliott's observations, we recognize that regular 5-wave patterns are important, because the end of a regular 5-wave swing pattern is often the point of a major trend reversal in the market.

Exercise 4–A:

On the chart of the S&P500 Index (Figure 4.3), complete the following two tasks:

(a) **Find and mark a regular 5-wave price pattern, where the beginning of the price pattern is marked #0, the end of the first wave is marked #1, the end of the second wave is set to #2, and so on.**

(b) **Draw the upper and lower channel lines.**

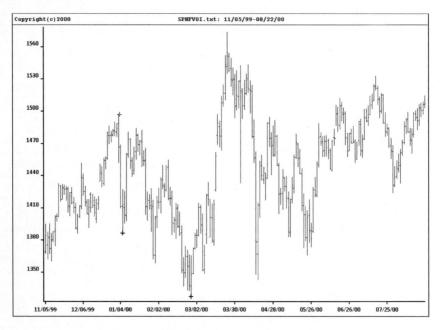

Figure 4.3   S&P500 Index from 11–99 to 08–00.

Regular 5-wave price patterns appear only on rare occasions. Most of the time, peaks #1, #3, and #5 will not be on the same line because market-price moves are generally irregular.

Irregular price moves do not show up in the first three waves of a 5-wave price pattern because we always have an initial 3-swing

pattern at the beginning of impulse waves or corrections in an uptrend or a downtrend. Irregular price patterns in a 5-wave price move
can be analyzed, after the first 3-wave pattern is completed, with a
modified trend channel analysis.

We can instantly identify an irregular price pattern. First, we
draw a line, through peak #1, that is parallel to the connection of valley #0 and valley #2. If peak #3 is not on this line, we are dealing with
an irregular price pattern. To capture the peak at point #5, we draw
a line through the valley at point #2 and point #4, and then add to this
line a parallel line that runs through peak #3.

Figure 4.4 illustrates how to define a trend channel, even if
we have an irregular market price pattern for a 5-wave move to the
upside.

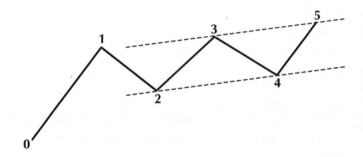

Figure 4.4   Trend channel with an irregular peak in an uptrend.

Irregular price patterns happen more often than regular price
patterns. It is a bit more difficult to integrate them on a chart, but
using them can help in identifying the end of a 5-wave market price
pattern.

Exercise 4–B:
**On the chart of the S&P500 Index (Figure 4.5), complete
the following three tasks:**

(a) **Find and mark an irregular 5-wave price pattern.**

(b) **Draw the parallel to the line that connects valley #0 and
valley #2 through peak #1.**

(c) Draw the parallel to the line that connects valley #2 and valley #4 through peak #3.

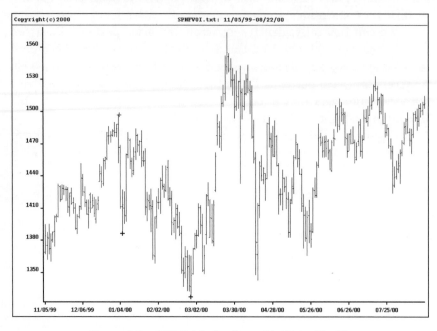

SPHFVOI.txt: 11/05/99-08/22/00

Figure 4.5   S&P500 Index from 11–99 to 08–00.

STRUCTURE OF PHI-CHANNELS

In Chapters 2 and 3, we utilized the numbers of the Fibonacci summation series as instruments to forecast possible major trend changes in time, and then analyzed corrections and extensions as Fibonacci tools to forecast trend changes in price.

PHI-channels, as geometric Fibonacci trading devices, are different from the plain numbers of the Fibonacci summation series, as well as from corrections and extensions, because they are able to identify support and resistance points in price and time simultaneously.

PHI-channels vary from regular trend channels in distinct ways. They have the same initial pattern structure as regular trend channels, and a 3-wave price move, but instead of isolating the outside points, PHI-channels are based on peak-to-valley and valley-to-peak connections.

The baseline of a PHI-channel can be generated out of a 3-wave market move, as shown in Figure 4.6.

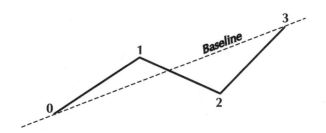

Figure 4.6   Baseline of a PHI-channel. *Source:* FAM Research, 2000.

The baseline of a PHI-channel is the connection of the price move from the bottom (at point #0) to the top (at point #3). Once the baseline is established, we draw a parallel line to the baseline, using the low at point #2 as our outside point to the right side of the price pattern. The distance from the baseline to the parallel line is the width of the PHI-channel.

Regular trend channels are turned into PHI-channels by using the width of the PHI-channel from the PHI-channel baseline to the outside parallel line, and multiplying this distance by the Fibonacci ratios of 0.618, 1.000, 1.618, 2.618, 4.236, and so on, for the width of the PHI-channel.

The resulting PHI-channel parallel lines are designed to work as trend indicators for market moves, once market pricing leaves the PHI-channel.

PHI-channel trend parallels that are derived from the connection of impulse waves are indications of support and resistance levels for price action in the direction of the main trend. The procedure of adding outside parallels in distances from the Fibonacci ratios is shown in Figure 4.7.

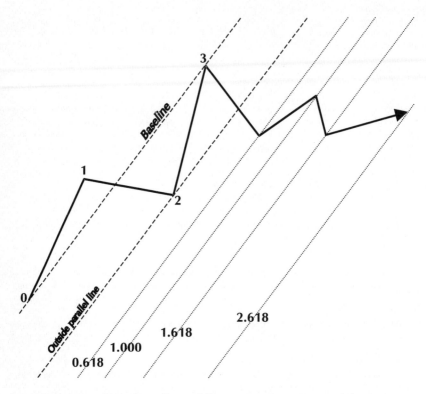

Figure 4.7   PHI-channel trend lines. *Source:* **FAM Research, 2000.**

It is also possible to draw PHI-channels from corrective waves in a price pattern. PHI-channels based on corrections provide us with resistance levels counter to the main trend direction. In this type of PHI-channel, baselines are determined by the high or low at point #3 and the low or high at point #6 in a 4–5–6 corrective move.

Figure 4.8 contrasts the generation of PHI-channel resistance lines out of corrective market movements counter to the main trend direction with the generation of PHI-channel support lines for the main trend.

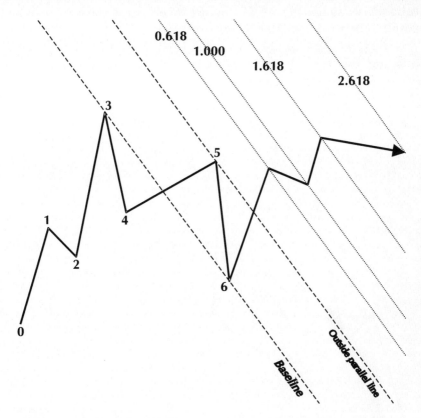

Figure 4.8   PHI-channel resistance lines. *Source:* FAM Research, 2000.

PHI-channel trend lines that are drawn parallel to the main trend direction can be combined with PHI-channel resistance lines drawn parallel to corrections counter to the main trend. The result is a cobweb of trend lines and resistance lines based on different Fibonacci ratios.

All crossover points of trend lines and resistance lines out of a PHI-channel are where future price moves may find support or resistance.

Crossover points of trend lines and resistance lines are determined by the number of ratios used from the PHI-series. Therefore,
only major peaks and major valleys in the market can be regarded as
valid when calculating a PHI-channel baseline and the corresponding
parallel lines outside the PHI-channel.

Figure 4.9 shows the crossovers from the combination of trend
lines and resistance lines out of a PHI-channel.

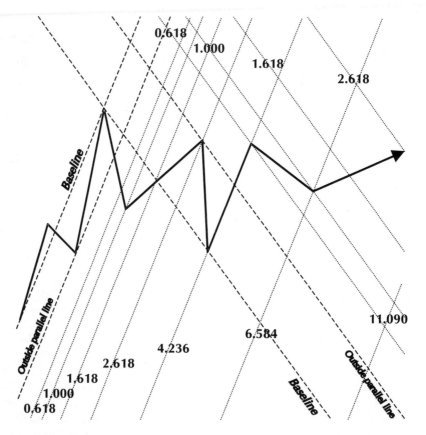

Figure 4.9   PHI-channel trend lines and resistance lines combined. *Source:*
FAM Research, 2000.

A projection of future investor behavior in price and time is seen
by generating crossovers of PHI-channel trend lines parallel to a main

trend, and PHI-channel resistance lines as countertrend lines to the main trend. Because we rely on high/low to low/high connections, angles of PHI-channels will vary a lot, but it does not really matter whether a PHI-channel runs steep or flat. What is important about PHI-channels is that peak-and-valley formations have a major impact on price moves in the future. This is the only way to explain why, in many instances, PHI-channel lines serve as support and resistance lines with such stunning accuracy.

We may never know which line will be reached and when crossover points will be triggered, but trend lines and resistance lines from PHI-channels are very significant when confirming buy and sell signals, especially when used with other Fibonacci tools.

PHI-channel support and resistance lines are often expressions of perfect symmetry within price patterns. This is in contrast to regular trend channels, which do not have the built-in flexibility to adjust quickly enough to changing price patterns and, thus, are of less forecasting value.

The use of prominent peaks and valleys for the calculation of PHI-channels combined with the Fibonacci ratios shows that price moves are not random. Price patterns, by themselves, can be predicted if analyzed correctly. The secret of PHI-channels is to identify which valleys and peaks to use. Once we have detected the appropriate peaks and valleys in the market, support and resistance lines can be drawn weeks and months into the future.

Identifying the appropriate PHI-channel is not difficult, for close market observation reveals how market pricing may or may not use the cobweb formation as support or resistance. Once the first line is triggered, the relevance of the PHI-channel lines drawn at higher Fibonacci ratios is confirmed.

PHI-channels that have been correctly identified, and parallels that have been properly calculated, often follow Elliott's rule of alternation, which is a very important pattern in nature. Whenever an outer parallel is triggered, prices move back toward the line drawn at the preceding ratio from the PHI-series. This happens before a move to the next outer line begins.

Still another factor points to the findings of Elliott. When a trend line is not touched but is strongly broken and is followed by a trend reversal, market pricing will penetrate the next PHI-channel line in most cases. This correlates with Elliott's claim that when a market price exceeds a number in the Fibonacci series in time, we can expect that the next number in the Fibonacci summation series will also be reached.

WORKING WITH PHI-CHANNELS

Trend channels are transformed into PHI-channels when parallel lines are no longer drawn from peak to peak and from valley to valley. Instead, a PHI-channel baseline is established by the peak-to-valley and valley-to-peak connection of the first and the second impulse waves. Once the baseline is established, a parallel line through the outside point of the price pattern determines the width of the PHI-channel. PHI-channel trend lines are calculated by multiplying the width of the PHI-channel by the Fibonacci ratios.

PHI-Channel Trend Lines

In the next exercise, we will demonstrate that PHI-channels are as easy to draw as regular trend lines.

If the width of the PHI-channel is 1.000, the next PHI-channel line with the measurement 1.000 will be parallel to the PHI-channel in the distance of the width of the PHI-channel, and the following channel lines will be at distances 1.618, 2.618, 4.236, and so on.

Exercise 4–C:

In the chart of the S&P500 Index in Figure 4.10, we have marked the significant peaks and valleys from #0 to #13. Draw the PHI-channel trend lines following three steps:

(a) Draw the baseline of the first PHI-channel.

(b) Draw the outside parallel to establish the PHI-channel.

(c) Draw PHI-channel lines using the Fibonacci ratios 1.000, 1.618, 2.618, and 4.236.

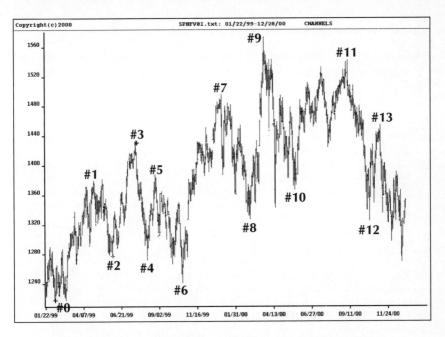

Figure 4.10   The S&P500 Index from 01–99 to 12–00.

PHI-Channel Resistance Lines

Instead of connecting the valley at point #0 with the peak at point #3 to establish the PHI-channel trend lines, the baseline of the PHI-channel out of the correction (as the basis for generating PHI-channel resistance lines) is drawn so that it intersects an imaginary line running from the valley at point #2 to the following peak at point #3.

This new baseline connects the significant peak #1 and the significant valley #6 in Figure 4.11 to generate the PHI-channel resistance lines.

Exercise 4–D:

Based on the above information, complete this exercise using the chart of the S&P500 Index in Figure 4.11:

(a) **Draw the outside line for the PHI-channel.**

(b) **Draw the PHI-channel resistance lines, based on the width of the PHI-channel and using the Fibonacci ratios 1.000, 1.618, and 2.618.**

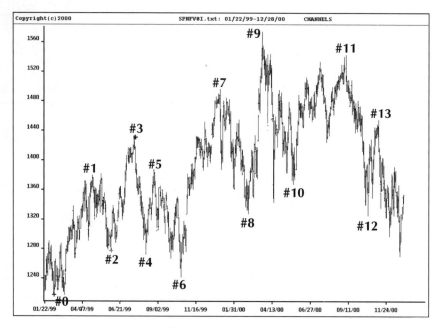

Figure 4.11   S&P500 Index from 01–99 to 12–00.

Working with PHI-channels requires a long-term analysis of market price action. The shorter the compression of the data, the more difficult it is to identify the significant peaks and valleys that create the basic structure of the PHI-channels.

PHI-channel analysis works very well on the S&P500 Index, but we will now present the DAX30 Index to show readers that the application of PHI-channels as Fibonacci tools is not limited to the United States of America. PHI-channel analysis works worldwide on any product with volatility and high market participation.

Applying PHI-Channels to the DAX30 Index

The DAX30 Index, like the S&P500 Index, is a very liquid and volatile trading device. Its market price moves in rhythms, and significant peaks and valleys are easily identified.

In Figure 4.12, we have charted the DAX30 Index for 31 months, from June 1998 to December 2000, in a cobweb design of PHI-channel trend lines and PHI-channel resistance lines.

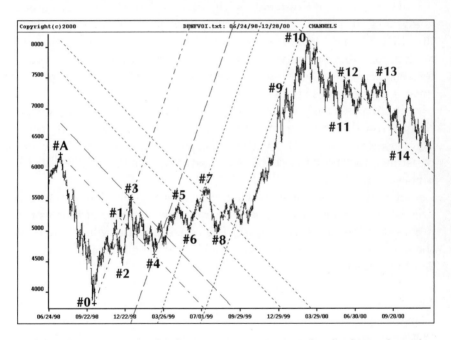

Figure 4.12   DAX30 Index from 06–98 to 12–00. Cobweb of PHI-channel trend lines and PHI-channel resistance lines. *Source:* FAM Research, 2000.

The DAX30 Index triggered a significant low at 3,810.00 on October 8, 1998. This valley is our starting point (#0), and it is the baseline of the first PHI-channel. The underlying pattern marks an impulse wave in an uptrend. Peak #3 of the 3-wave uptrend price pattern, following the lowest low, is connected to the valley at point #0 and marks the ending point of the PHI-channel baseline. The parallel to the baseline is drawn through the outside valley at point #4.

The resulting width of the PHI-channel, multiplied by the ratio 0.618, leads us to a PHI-channel trend line that acts as a support-and-resistance line for the valley (at point #6) and the peak (at point #7). Even more important, the PHI-channel trend line, generated at a ratio of 1.618, is the resistance line for a strong uptrend when peak #9 touches the PHI-channel line. This all occurs just as the DAX30 Index is on its way up from a level of 5,000.0 to a highest high: above 8,136.0 points.

This finding corresponds with what we have learned from our analysis of the S&P500 Index market movements. Thus, we conclude that PHI-channels can serve as trend lines and resistance lines, depending on whether we work with peak-to-valley formations (countertrend lines) or valley-to-peak formations (trend lines) in an uptrend (vice versa in a downtrend).

It surprises researchers, analysts, and traders alike, that a PHI-channel line drawn at a ratio 11.090 parallel to the baseline, connecting a peak in 1998 and a valley in 1999, creates a level of perfect resistance for the DAX30 Index almost one year later (2000) at its highest high.

It is also quite amazing that the same PHI-channel resistance line defines the median line of the strong downtrend that follows the highest high in the DAX30 Index. The resistance line, which starts at the peak (point #10), intersects the imaginary connection from valley #11 to peak #13.

To trace the price movements of the DAX30 Index after the highest high above 8,000.0 points in March 2000, we have the option of drawing either PHI-channel trend lines, using a baseline in the direction of the main trend, or PHI-channel resistance lines, using a baseline out of a market correction counter to the main trend.

The PHI-channel can easily be drawn by hand. Readers who have the WINPHI software package can use the historical data on the DAX30 Index and draw the PHI-channel lines with the WINPHI program.

Exercise 4–E:
In the chart of the DAX30 Index (Figure 4.13), we have marked the valley in September 1998 as #0, and numbered the significant peaks and valleys as peak #1, valley #2, and peak #3. Based on the numbered peaks and valleys, complete these two tasks:

(a) Draw the PHI-channel.

(b) Draw the PHI-channel trend lines using the ratios 0.618, 1.000, and 1.618.

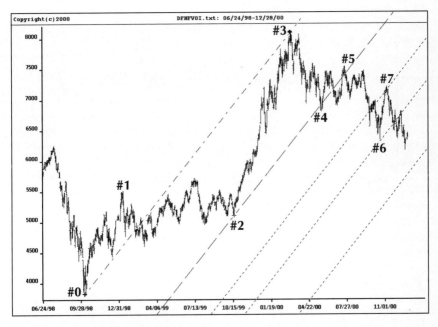

Figure 4.13   DAX30 Index from 06–98 to 12–00.

The DAX30 Index price action (following the all-time high in March 2000) can also be captured by resistance lines, generated on the basis of a PHI-channel analysis.

Exercise 4–F:

In the chart of the DAX30 Index in Figure 4.14, complete the following steps:

(a) **Draw the outside parallel line of the PHI-channel through point #3, using the initial baseline of the PHI-channel that follows the correction from the major peak at point #1 to the major valley at point #4.**

(b) **Draw the set of PHI-channel resistance lines by multiplying the width of the PHI-channel by the PHI-ratios 2.618 and 4.236.**

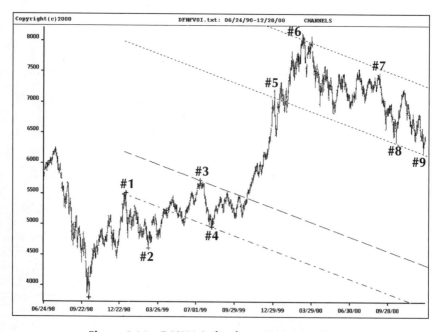

Figure 4.14   DAX30 Index from 06–98 to 12–00.

Because the distances from the baseline to valley #2 and the baseline to peak #3 are almost identical, a very symmetrical pattern of market behavior can be identified, just as in Exercise 4–E.

ANSWERS TO EXERCISES

This chapter has provided an introduction to PHI-channels. A full description is given in the textbook, on pages 105–136. Each exercise can be reproduced with the WINPHI program and its historical data, or online at **www.fibotrader.com.**

Exercise 4–A:

A perfect example of a regular 5-wave price pattern is shown in Figure 4.15, a chart of the S&P500 Index in late 1999 and early 2000.

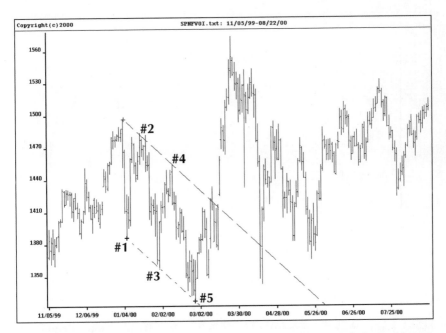

Figure 4.15   S&P500 Index from 11–99 to 08–00. Regular trend channel in a 5-wave pattern. *Source:* **FAM Research, 2000.**

The market pattern in the S&P500 Index between December 1999 and March 2000 is perfect because market pricing has moved in a regular 5-wave swing, exactly inside our trend channel, for over three months.

The significant valley at point #5, at a low of 1,327.00, was a major trend reversal to the upside. The S&P500 Index then moved straight up, 247 points, to the highest high: 1,574.00 in March 2000.

Exercise 4–B:

If we want to invest countertrend, it always pays to wait for the end of a 5-wave price pattern, regardless of whether it is a regular or an irregular price move.

In Figure 4.16, we show an irregular 5-wave price pattern in the S&P500 Index.

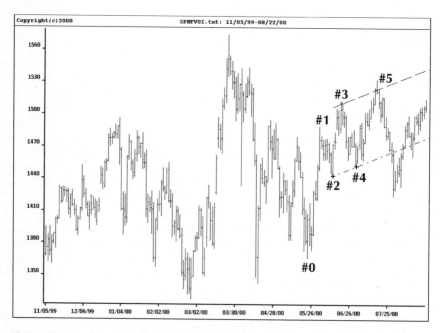

Figure 4.16   S&P500 Index from 11–99 to 08–00. A trend channel in an irregular 5-wave pattern. *Source:* FAM Research, 2000.

Exercises 4–C, 4–D:

In exercises 4–C and 4–D, we are working with PHI-channel trend lines and resistance lines. In the S&P500 Index chart in Figure 4.17, the answers to both exercises are combined. The turning points are the same as those marked in Figures 4.10 and 4.11.

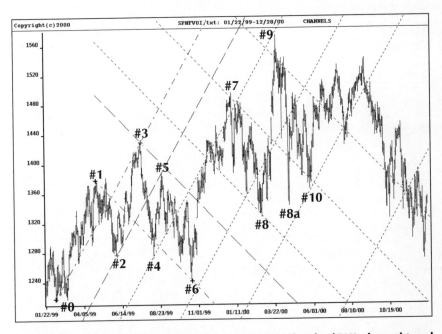

Figure 4.17   S&P500 Index from 01–99 to 12–00. Cobweb of PHI-channel trend lines and PHI-channel resistance lines. *Source:* **FAM Research, 2000.**

Looking at Figure 4.17, one easily recognizes that the S&P500 Index market price reached its highest high with the peak at point #9. This major trend reversal was well captured by the crossover of a PHI-channel trend line and a PHI-channel resistance line.

Exercises 4–E, 4–F:

In the chart of the DAX30 Index in Figure 4.18, we combine exercises 4–E and 4–F to demonstrate the generation of support and resistance lines.

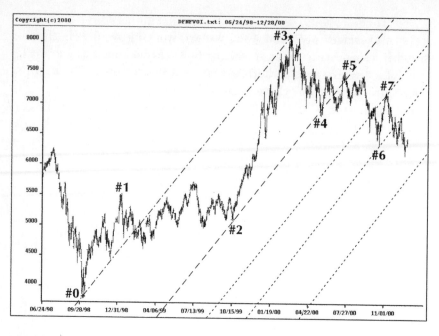

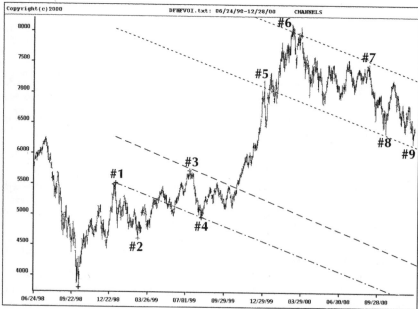

Figure 4.18   DAX30 Index from 06–98 to 12–00. *Source:* FAM Research, 2000.

PHI-channel analysis provides us with a multitude of options for setting baselines and parallel lines of different PHI-channels, and for drawing support and resistance lines from them.

The overall usefulness of PHI-channel trend lines and resistance lines will, however, vary from case to case. For example, we may start our PHI-channel analysis at the highest high ever traded in the DAX30 Index. We could also reduce the time period analyzed and start in January 2000 instead of June 1998.

In Figure 4.19, we map the market situation in the DAX30 Index in a cobweb design from a price data chart sample pointing into the year 2001 (Figure 4.19).

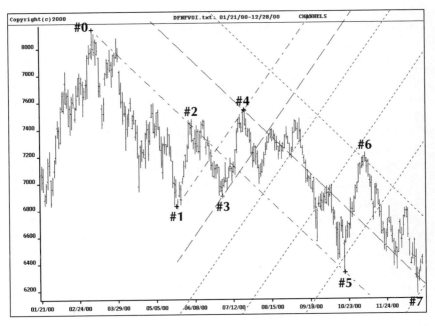

Figure 4.19 DAX30 Index from 01–00 to 12–00. Cobweb of PHI-channel trend lines and PHI-channel resistance lines. *Source:* FAM Research, 2000.

The impulse wave baseline is established from the peak at point #0 to the valley at point #5, with an outside parallel line drawn through the peak at point #4.

The PHI-channel resistance line is defined by multiplying the width of the PHI-channel, from the baseline to the parallel outside line, by the ratio 1.000. This PHI-channel line is the resistance line for the market price. The peak at point #6 on the DAX30 Index chart appeared when the PHI-channel resistance line was penetrated. The second baseline following a corrective move is established by connecting the valley at point #1 and the peak at point #4. The PHI-channel is completed by choosing the parallel line through valley #3. PHI-channel trend lines are then created based on the Fibonacci ratios 1.000, 1.618, 2.618, and 4.236.

By now, readers know more about the actual price moves of the DAX30 Index than we knew in December 2000, and they will see how valuable our analysis (with the help of the WINPHI software) has been.

FINAL REMARKS

Investor behavior expresses itself in chart patterns, trend formations, sideward markets, and peaks and valleys. Every significant peak or valley can be seen as an indication of what the majority of investors expect in the market at any moment in time.

Our analysis focuses on daily data because intraday peaks or valleys are not as meaningful as those that occur daily or weekly, but the analysis can easily be extended to sets of weekly data as well.

Significant peaks and valleys in the markets are much more relevant than traders realize. Trend channels are generated by establishing major peak-to-peak or valley-to-valley connections out of regular 3-wave or 5-wave market moves. This is why trend channels should be the primary step when analyzing markets.

PHI-channels are more effective trading tools than regular trend channels, and are generated slightly differently. Our PHI-channel analysis works with baselines as connections of significant high-to-low and low-to-high formations.

PHI-channels can be drawn from either impulse waves or corrective waves, and by determining the outside parallel line of a PHI-channel. The parallel line is determined by the next significant peak or valley to the right of the baseline. As soon as a PHI-channel has been established, the width of the PHI-channel (measured by the distance from the baseline to the parallel outside line) can be multiplied by the Fibonacci ratios 0.618, 1.000, 1.618, 2.618, 4.236, and so on. Depending on which peaks or valleys are used, the PHI-channel lines can be either trend lines or resistance lines.

How can correct PHI-channels be distinguished from false ones? If the first major turning point in the market (after the PHI-channel is drawn) finds its support and resistance in the first PHI-channel trend line or resistance line, drawn at Fibonacci ratios 0.618 and 1.000 (at the most), then it is a correct PHI-channel. Once this condition is met, we can be sure that the next PHI-channel lines drawn at higher ratios from the PHI-series will be important support or resistance lines as well.

PHI-channel lines can only be drawn with the WINPHI software package. Readers are referred to the User Manual in *The New Fibonacci Trader* for advice on how to recognize and fully utilize PHI-channel trend lines and resistance lines.

Using PHI-channel lines is an excellent way to map out price actions and to make investor behavior visible. Market swings can be followed up and down like a road map, as long as the correct PHI-channel lines are selected.

5

PHI-ELLIPSES

In Chapter 4, we described the risk of working with peak and valley formations in 3-wave and 5-wave patterns. Because swing formations are easy to identify and to integrate into computerized trading environments, peak and valley formations are often used, especially by traders or managers who invest in smaller accounts. Many profitable trades can be made, as long as there are regular wave patterns and each impulse wave defines new highs or new lows by a wide margin. However, in multiple corrections with many false breakouts, swing systems are of little use because they are based only on price analysis.

Product analysis changes as soon as we add *time* to the equation. Adding the time element to an analysis of market movements brings more stability to investment strategies. This is where the PHI-ellipse becomes valuable, for it is one of the few investment tools that can identify turning points based on the Fibonacci ratios in price and time.

Working with PHI-ellipses is not easy. Their basic structure is simple, but because price patterns change over time, the final shape of a PHI-ellipse may vary markedly. The application of PHI-ellipses may seem confusing at first because there are different forms and wave structures within a PHI-ellipse, and different PHI-ellipses can sometimes be linked together. It takes a lot of skill to properly work with PHI-ellipses as investment tools, but this skill can be developed with practice.

This introduction to PHI-ellipses is only the tip of the iceberg, for ellipses are complex and the creative possibilities are endless. *The New Fibonacci Trader* goes into much more detail on PHI-ellipses on pages 138–194.

PHI-ellipses are conceptually rooted in the Fibonacci ratios. We can combine PHI-ellipses with other Fibonacci tools, such as the Fibonacci summation series, extensions and corrections, PHI-spirals, and Fibonacci time-goal days, which will be discussed in the following chapters. In Chapter 8, all of the Fibonacci tools are combined into one analytic trading tool.

BASIC FEATURES OF PHI-ELLIPSES

What makes PHI-ellipses so interesting is that they are able to identify underlying structures of price moves. PHI-ellipses circumvent price patterns. When a price pattern changes, the shape of the PHI-ellipse that circumvents the respective market price pattern changes. We find long and short PHI-ellipses, fat and thin PHI-ellipses, as well as PHI-ellipses that are flat or have a steep angle. Their slopes are determined by the high in downtrends and the low in uptrends of the correction wave 2 in our wave count. Their lengths are determined by the correction in wave 2 after the first impulse wave. These changing measurements determine the overall shape of the ellipse.

There are very few market price moves that do not follow the pattern of a PHI-ellipse.

PHI-ellipses are important analytical instruments when investing countertrend to market actions because, with them, we can see whether a price move stays within the PHI-ellipse and invest accordingly if a price move breaks out of a PHI-ellipse at the very end.

Looking backward on historical charts, one finds that very few price moves in commodities, futures, stock index futures, or stocks show up that cannot be circumvented with a PHI-ellipse. However, finding the correct PHI-ellipse is an art. It takes skill, experience, patience, and trust to effectively utilize PHI-ellipses as Fibonacci investment tools.

It is impossible to forecast the final shape of a PHI-ellipse at the beginning of a price move. As we will show, PHI-ellipses may follow one after the other, often in different shapes and varying sizes. The investor's challenge is to correctly interpret price moves and select PHI-ellipses accordingly. Once the appropriate market price pattern has been identified, working with PHI-ellipses becomes very easy.

PHI-Ellipses as Investment Tools

Unlike any other investment tool available today, PHI-ellipses give a solid overall picture of the total price pattern. PHI-ellipses are the perfect geometric Fibonacci trading tools to cope with the "noise" in price patterns and to analyze price moves as entities over time. The generation of PHI-ellipses is best demonstrated by starting with a circle and then turning the circle into PHI-ellipses.

A circle is a special kind of PHI-ellipse in that the ratio of the major and minor axes is 1.000 from the Fibonacci ratios. From the circle, ongoing PHI-ellipses can be drawn at alternative major to minor axes, Fibonacci ratios, such as 1.618, 2.618, 4.236, 6.854, 11.090, 17.944, and so on.

In the textbook, *The New Fibonacci Trader,* we coin the concept of a "Fischer-transformed" PHI-ellipse, which is distinct from commonly known ellipses. As explained in Chapter 1, the regular ellipse quickly turns into a "Havana cigar" with each increasing Fibonacci number, whereas our transformed PHI-ellipse holds its shape much longer and is, therefore, better for analyzing price data.

Figure 5.1 shows the generation of PHI-ellipses starting with a circle and then successively increasing the axis ratios.

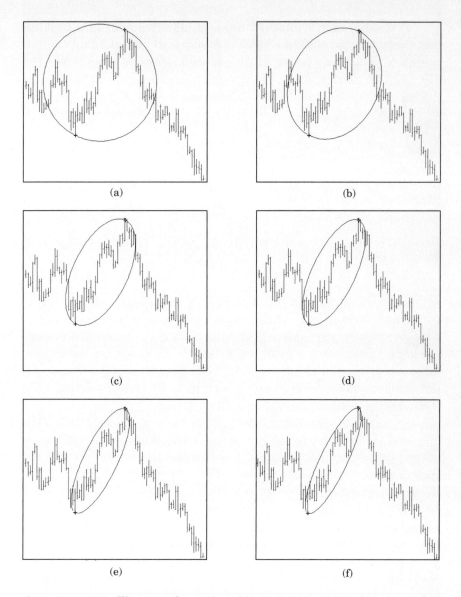

Figure 5.1   PHI-ellipses at alternative ratios. (a) Ratio 1.000; (b) ratio 1.618; (c) ratio 4.236; (d) ratio 6.854; (e) ratio 11.090; (f) ratio 17.944. *Source:* FAM Research, 2000.

PHI-ellipses are interesting as graphic trading tools because their structure is founded on a 3-wave pattern (Figure 5.2).

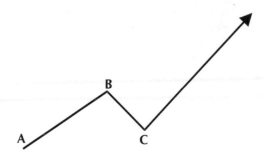

Figure 5.2 **General structure of a 3-wave pattern.** *Source:* FAM Research, 2000.

Once the three points A, B, and C in the 3-wave swing are identified, we can position the PHI-ellipse around them. Wave 1, from A to B, is an impulse wave. Wave 2, from B to C, is the corrective wave to the impulse wave. For wave 3, we expect a second impulse wave in the direction of the first impulse wave. This general pattern follows Elliott's wave principles and can be seen in every traded product, be it commodities, futures, stocks, or cash currencies.

Tracking the changes in the fundamental structure of the PHI-ellipse is another way to analyze price moves. What makes ellipses so unique is that they are dynamic over time and follow price patterns as they develop. This is why we must always be patient and wait—from the very beginning to the very end—to see whether a price move stays within the PHI-ellipse. Action can be taken as soon as the market price moves out of the PHI-ellipse, but only if the price pattern has run completely inside a PHI-ellipse until the final point.

As a general rule, if the angle of a PHI-ellipse is sloping upward, we can sell at the end of the PHI-ellipse. If the slope of the PHI-ellipse is downward, we can buy at the end of the PHI-ellipse. The exception to this rule will be described later.

It is very important to remember that PHI-ellipses are not means of forecasting market moves. We never know in advance whether a price move will stay within the PHI-ellipse and reach its end. Before taking action, we must always wait to see whether a price move stays inside the border of the PHI-ellipse.

There is no standard PHI-ellipse that suits every product. To work with PHI-ellipses as investment tools, we must identify the minimum length and minimum thickness of relevant PHI-ellipses for every single product, because every product traded has its own characteristic price behavior. This price behavior expresses itself in a price pattern, which can only be identified on the basis of historical charts.

Working with a PHI-ellipse tells us where we are in the price action at any point in time. Whenever a trend reverses at the end of a PHI-ellipse, we can attach PHI-ellipses and take the final point of an old PHI-ellipse as the beginning of a new PHI-ellipse.

Whenever market price action moves out of the PHI-ellipse before reaching the final point of the PHI-ellipse (either to the upside or to the downside), we can assume that we are at the beginning of a new market price pattern that might fit into a new PHI-ellipse. In addition to attaching PHI-ellipses, we might find PHI-ellipses that overlap (Figure 5.3).

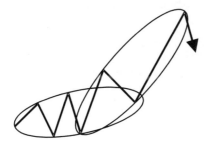

Figure 5.3   Overlapping PHI-ellipses. *Source:* FAM Research, 2000.

The slope of a PHI-ellipse is a parameter that cannot be underestimated. The slope of PHI-ellipses first determines the profit potential of countertrend trading signals. Figure 5.4 shows different profit potentials in relation to the slope of underlying PHI-ellipses.

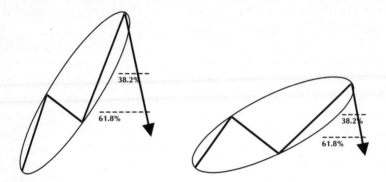

Figure 5.4 Profit potential based on the slope of PHI-ellipses. *Source:* FAM Research, 2000.

Simultaneously analyzing the weekly and daily data on the same product is often very beneficial to the outcome of the analysis. For instance, recognizing a PHI-ellipse with a strong uptrend from weekly data will help identify the correct trading signal based on daily data.

Figure 5.5 illustrates the incorporation of daily data into the longer-term weekly picture.

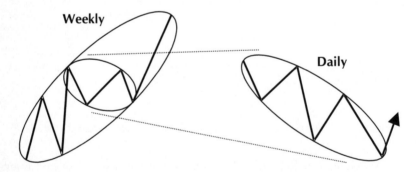

Figure 5.5 Simultaneous analysis on weekly and daily PHI-ellipses. *Source:* FAM Research, 2000.

Entry Rules

The basic strategy for using PHI-ellipses when trading the markets is: (1) wait for a price move to develop inside the border of a PHI-ellipse and (2) act counter to the main trend direction as soon as the end of the PHI-ellipse has been reached and the market price moves out of the PHI-ellipse.

Catching the rhythm of market movements by attaching PHI-ellipses and adding countertrend trades to each other is illustrated in Figure 5.6.

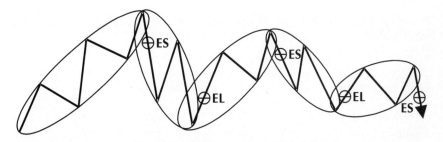

Figure 5.6   Basic scheme of investment using PHI-ellipses. *Source:* **FAM Research, 2000.**

Selling at the end of a PHI-ellipse is recommended when the PHI-ellipse has an upward slope. Buying at the end of a PHI-ellipse is recommended when the PHI-ellipse has a downward slope. There are two ways we can sell at an entry signal:

1. Sell at the point where the market price moves out of the right side of the PHI-ellipse.

2. Sell when the market price moves out of the right side of the PHI-ellipse and also breaks the low of the previous one, two, three, or four days.

The entry rule chosen by investors depends on their risk preference and how early they want to be invested.

Figure 5.7 shows a sell signal where the market price has moved out of the right side of the PHI-ellipse and a previous four-day low is broken.

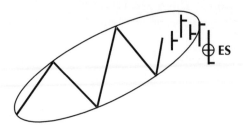

Figure 5.7   A four-day lowest-low entry rule on PHI-ellipses. *Source:* FAM Research, 2000.

Stop-Loss Rules

As soon as we are invested on a short position, we define a stop-loss or a stop-reverse point at the highest high of a price bar within the previous PHI-ellipse. If we are invested long, we protect our position with a stop-loss at the lowest low of a price bar within the previous PHI-ellipse.

Figure 5.8 covers the stop-loss rule for an investment short out of a PHI-ellipse.

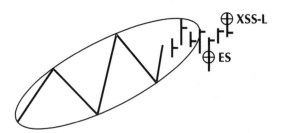

Figure 5.8   Stop-loss protection on a short position. *Source:* FAM Research, 2000.

For an alternative selling point, we may also consider the trend channel that touches the relevant PHI-ellipse on either side.

By choosing the conservative option of a double confirmation by PHI-ellipse and trend channel, we accept that we might give up some profit potential that could have been realized by acting upon a more sensitive entry rule. On the other hand, we might avoid a number of losing trades in strong trending conditions by staying in the trend channel as long as it lasts (Figure 5.9).

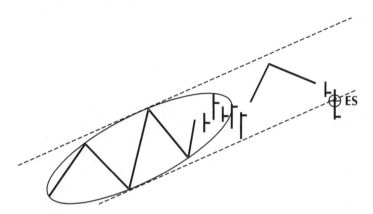

Figure 5.9 Short entry on PHI-ellipse and trend channel combined. *Source:* **FAM Research, 2000.**

Trailing Stop Rules

The most conservative strategy for protecting an existing profit is to work with a trailing stop at the previous four days' high (or low). In most cases, this option protects at least part of the profits, although it also means giving away open profits (Figure 5.10).

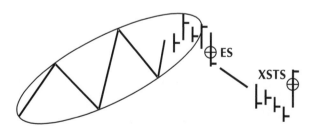

Figure 5.10 Trailing stop exit on previous four days' high. *Source:* **FAM Research, 2000.**

Profit Target Rules

There are different ways to work with profit targets. One way to define a profit target price level is to work with a 50.0% or 61.8% retracement level set by the lowest low and the highest high of the previous PHI-ellipse.

Another option is to wait until the market price reaches the end of a new PHI-ellipse. This exit rule requires the most patience and the strongest discipline, but it also has the biggest profit potential of the different exit rules (Figure 5.11).

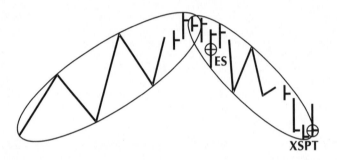

Figure 5.11   Profit target exit on the end of a PHI-ellipse. *Source:* FAM Research, 2000.

WORKING WITH PHI-ELLIPSES

Working with PHI-ellipses is easy if we understand the rationale behind their basic structure.

PHI-ellipses develop over time. The PHI-ellipse form exists inherently from the beginning, but, as investors, we can only utilize PHI-ellipses at the very end. Although all PHI-ellipses share a common key-structure, their final forms vary, becoming thick or thin, long or short. They can be single manifestations of smaller trend moves or part of a circumvented major trend.

Question 5–1:
What determines the shape of a PHI-ellipse?

Question 5–2:
What is the major difference between the price patterns of the two PHI-ellipses shown in Figure 5.12?

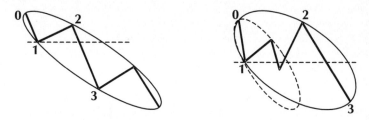

Figure 5.12 Adjustment of PHI-ellipses based on the duration of corrections. *Source:* FAM Research, 2000.

We work with PHI-ellipses to analyze market patterns. Investing with PHI-ellipses means waiting until the price move reaches the very end of the PHI-ellipse. The question is: Where is the end of a PHI-ellipse?

To answer this question, we must combine the PHI-ellipse with other Fibonacci trading tools. PHI-ellipses circumvent price patterns and show investors "where we are" in a price move, but the integration of other Fibonacci devices makes trading even safer.

Exercise 5–A:
In the chart of the Japanese Yen cash currency (Figure 5.13), we have marked the turning points A, B, C, C1, and D. Complete the following three tasks:

(a) **Explain why the outside of the PHI-ellipse touches C1 and not C.**

(b) **Mark the entry point of the buy long signal.**

(c) **Mark the point of the exit signal if we work with a trailing stop of four days.**

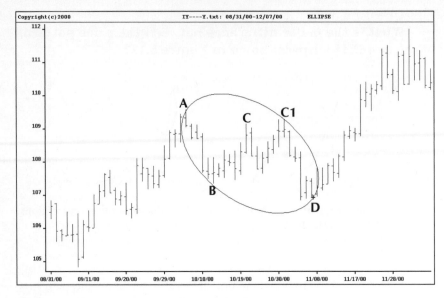

Figure 5.13 Japanese Yen cash currency from 08–00 to 12–00. *Source:* FAM Research, 2000.

Exercise 5–B:

In Chapter 4, we discussed the relevance of regular trend channels (as peak-to-peak and valley-to-valley connections) to analyze market patterns.

In the daily chart of the S&P500 Index from November 1999 to March 2000 (Figure 5.14), we combine trend channel analysis with the PHI-ellipse.

Complete the following three tasks:

(a) Mark the 5-wave regular trend channel that runs in the same direction as the PHI-ellipse.

(b) Mark the entry signal to buy long after the final point of the PHI-ellipse is reached.

(c) If we work with a trailing stop of four days and a re-entry rule of four days, where are the exit and re-entry points? Mark them.

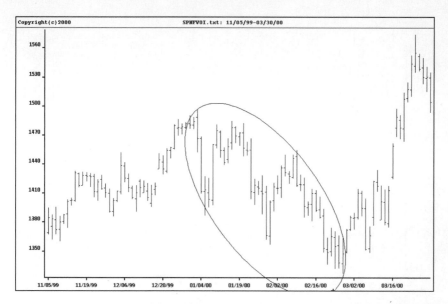

Figure 5.14   S&P500 Index from 11–99 to 03–00. *Source:* FAM Research, 2000.

The PHI-ellipse in Figure 5.15 is thinner and longer than the PHI-ellipses presented earlier. The reason for this difference is that the price pattern is a 5-wave move, not a 3-wave move. The first swing A to B and back to point C is established quickly, but a PHI-ellipse drawn around these swings has no stability at all.

Exercise 5–C:
On the chart of the Japanese Yen cash currency in Figure 5.15, complete the following three tasks:

(a) **Mark the 5-wave swing pattern.**

(b) **Draw the price band that defines the target corridor for an extension by using Fibonacci ratios: 1.618 for the amplitude of wave 1, and 0.618 for the amplitude of wave 3.**

(c) **Mark the entry signal to buy long, and mark the exit point based on a trailing stop rule of four days.**

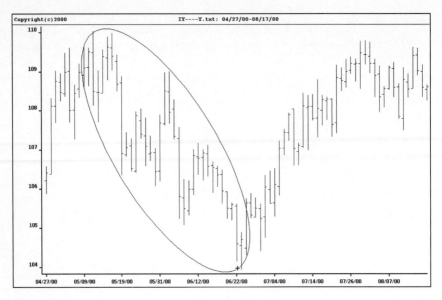

Figure 5.15 Japanese Yen cash currency from 04–00 to 08–00. *Source:* FAM Research, 2000.

In addition to combining PHI-ellipses with extensions, PHI-ellipses can easily be applied in combination with corrections as Fibonacci trading tools.

Exercise 5–D:
The PHI-ellipse shown on the S&P500 Index chart (Figure 5.16) has starting point A, side points B and O, and final point D as basic structural elements. To confirm the final point D, we must use additional Fibonacci tools.

Show how a price band can be created in Figure 5.16 to confirm the final point D of the PHI-ellipse:

(a) Mark the high and the low used to calculate the correction level of 61.8%, and draw the first line of the price band.

(b) Mark the high and the low of wave 1, then calculate the price band using the Fibonacci ratio 0.618, and draw the second line of the price band.

(c) **Mark the entry point to buy long.**

(d) **Mark the trailing stop level based on a four days' low exit
rule.**

(e) **Mark the entry point of a re-entry signal.**

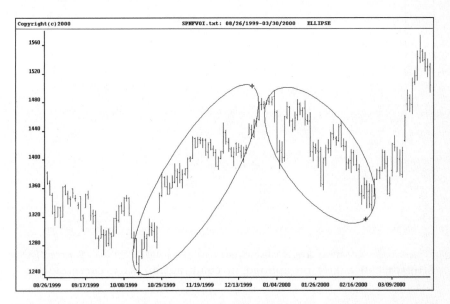

Figure 5.16   S&P500 Index from 08–99 to 03–00. *Source:* **FAM Research, 2000.**

The price pattern shown in Figure 5.17 is an example of the
Japanese Yen cash currency, between February 2000 and February
2001. The pattern is not seen often; it shows that the end of a PHI-
ellipse can indicate a trend change in the opposite direction, or a
breakout in the main trend direction.

In most cases, the market price reverses at the final point of the
PHI-ellipse, although the long-term picture in the Japanese Yen cash
currency shows otherwise. In this example, we see that after selling
short at point D, it is wise to reverse the position to the long side at the
final point of the PHI-ellipse. There is enough trading potential on
the upside (represented by the long-term PHI-ellipse), which is well

established and defined by the starting point in A and the side points in B and in C (Figure 5.17).

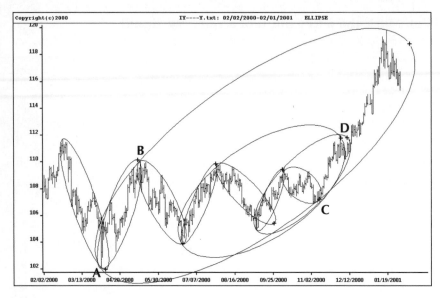

Figure 5.17   Japanese Yen cash currency from 02–00 to 02–01. *Source:* FAM Research, 2000.

Working with PHI-ellipses shows us that even the best-looking trading signals might turn out to be losing trades. As long as traders work with a solid stop-loss rule, any harm done by losing trades remains under control. To increase the profitability of investments, we highly recommend the combination of different Fibonacci devices.

ANSWERS TO QUESTIONS AND EXERCISES

In this workbook, we are concentrating on how to identify the basic structure of PHI-ellipses and how to integrate other Fibonacci trading tools.

The New Fibonacci Trader explains all these concepts, in full detail, on pages 137–194. All exercises can be reproduced by using the WINPHI graphics program and the historical database on CD-ROM.

Answer to Question 5–1:

The shape of the PHI-ellipse is determined by the Fibonacci ratio and the slope. With a change in the Fibonacci ratio, the shape of the PHI-ellipse becomes fatter or thinner. The slope of the PHI-ellipse is determined (in an uptrend) by the low of the correction wave 2 in our wave count. As long as the low of the correction wave 2 is above the low of wave 1, we will have three types of PHI-ellipses, as shown in Figure 5.18.

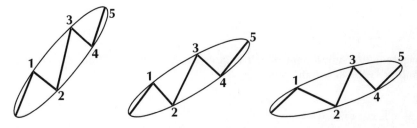

Figure 5.18 Slope of PHI-ellipses upward in relation to different correction levels. *Source:* FAM Research, 2000.

If the correction wave 2 goes below the starting point of wave 1, the slope of a PHI-ellipse will be neutral or will have a slope with a very small upward angle. This might be an indication of a sideward market (Figure 5.19).

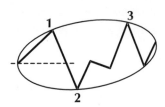

Figure 5.19 Slope of PHI-ellipses indicating a sideward market. *Source:* FAM Research, 2000.

Answer to Question 5–2:

For an ellipse to be a viable indication of a price pattern, wave 3 has to be longer than wave 1. This is the case in the first figure. In the second figure, we see that in order for wave 3 to be longer than wave 1, we have to adjust the width of the PHI-ellipse, so that wave 3 is the price swing from the high at point #2 to the low at point #3 (Figure 5.20).

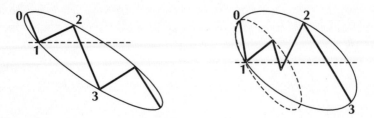

Figure 5.20 Adjustment of PHI-ellipses based on the duration of corrections. *Source:* FAM Research, 2000.

Exercise 5–A:

The basic structure of PHI-ellipses is always the same. To properly draw a PHI-ellipse, at least four points must be defined and touched by the borders of the PHI-ellipse. The four points are: (a) starting point, (b) left side, (c) right side, and (d) bottom of the PHI-ellipse.

The starting point is usually the highest or lowest point in a price move, but there are exceptions in patterns such as: (a) irregular tops or bottoms, (b) overlapping PHI-ellipses, and (c) very small angles in a PHI-ellipse.

The PHI-ellipse marked in Figure 5.21 consists of a simple 3-wave pattern. The starting point is A and the first of the two side points is B.

We can draw a PHI-ellipse through the peak at point C, but in order to complete a PHI-ellipse in a 3-wave pattern, the third wave has to go lower than point B. The price move does not go lower than point B after C is reached. Instead, it makes a higher high than C, and the side point changes from C to C1. This can happen any time we work with a PHI-ellipse. From C1, the price move goes quickly to point D.

However, at valley D, we do not know whether this is a low to watch, for even though we can already draw the PHI-ellipse through point D in its final form, we have to wait for the market price to go outside the PHI-ellipse at point F.

At point F in Figure 5.21, where market pricing leaves the PHI-ellipse, a trading signal is generated and executed based on the following parameters:

- Market entry on a breakout of the border of the PHI-ellipse;

- Stop-loss protection set to the lowest low before entry at the valley at point D;

- Trailing stop rule applied to protect profits, defined as a breakout of a previous four-day low, triggered at point G.

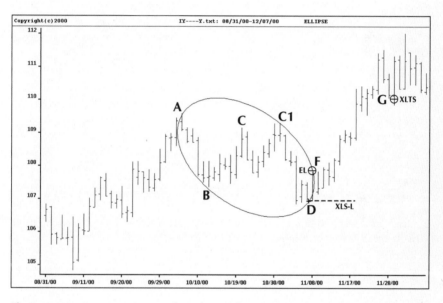

Figure 5.21 **Japanese Yen cash currency from 08–00 to 12–00.** *Source:* FAM Research, 2000. (Disclaimer: Past performance may not be indicative of future results.)

Exercise 5–B:
The starting point of the PHI-ellipse is at point A. The side points of the PHI-ellipse are B and O. The end point of the PHI-ellipse is reached at point D.

A trend channel is defined by the peaks at points C and O and a parallel drawn through the valley at point N. This parallel is almost penetrated by the price move at point D.

The buy signal is generated when the market price moves out of the right side of the PHI-ellipse. The trailing stop set at the previous four-day low is triggered at point E. The re-entry signal is established at point F with a second trailing stop executed at point G (Figure 5.22).

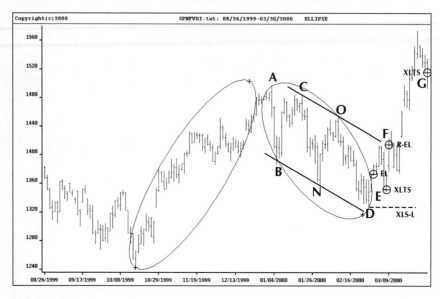

Figure 5.22   S&P500 Index from 08–99 to 03–00. *Source:* **FAM Research, 2000. (Disclaimer: Past performance may not be indicative of future results.)**

Exercise 5–C:

The PHI-ellipse in Figure 5.23 almost perfectly circumvents the 5-wave pattern in the Japanese Yen cash currency, but in order to identify the end, we must use the Fibonacci tools presented in Chapter 3.

The amplitude of wave 1 multiplied by the Fibonacci ratio 1.618, and the amplitude of wave 3 multiplied by the Fibonacci ratio 0.618, produce a price corridor that identifies the end of the PHI-ellipse.

The entry signal to buy long is reached as soon as the border of the PHI-ellipse is broken. The stop-loss protection is set to the valley at point F, which is the lowest low inside the PHI-ellipse. The trailing stop to protect the profit, defined as a breakout of a previous four-day low, is triggered at point G (Figure 5.23).

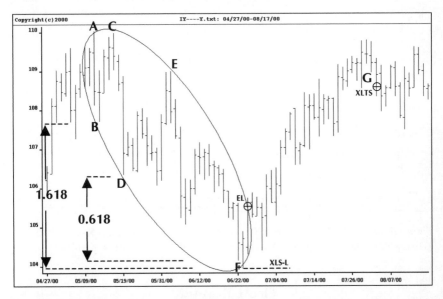

Figure 5.23 Japanese Yen cash currency from 04–00 to 08–00. *Source:* FAM Research, 2000. (Disclaimer: Past performance may not be indicative of future results.)

Exercise 5–D:

In Figure 5.24, the PHI-ellipse with the starting point in A and the final point in D is a correction of the price move shown in the PHI-ellipse. The swing size of this PHI-ellipse started at point X and reached its highest high at point A. The correction of 61.8% of the total amplitude between X and A is also the low of the new PHI-ellipse and creates the first line of the price band we are trying to find.

The amplitude between the peak at point A and the valley at point B, multiplied by the Fibonacci ratio 0.618, creates the second line of the price band.

The entry rule, stop-loss rule, re-entry rule, and trailing stop are the same as in Exercise 5–B.

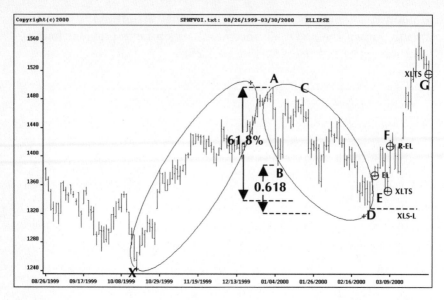

Figure 5.24   S&P500 Index from 08–99 to 03–00. *Source:* **FAM Research, 2000. (Disclaimer: Past performance may not be indicative of future results.)**

FINAL REMARKS

PHI-ellipses are special investment devices because they make chart patterns visible. When working with PHI-ellipses, investors will always know what to look for in the markets, regardless of how confusing daily, weekly, or monthly charts may appear.

The basic structure of the PHI-ellipse is simple. A PHI-ellipse circumvents a minimum of a 3-wave swing. To calculate PHI-ellipses, three points are needed: a starting point and two side points. The final point of a PHI-ellipse projects a future market move as the PHI-ellipse develops, and it is the decisive point to watch, whether it yields monthly, daily, or intraday data.

In the application of PHI-ellipses, investors are able to master trend patterns and sideward patterns. PHI-ellipses consist of three trading dimensions that are seldom found in a single trading tool: price, time, and angle. When a solid analysis of all three dimensions precalculates the same trading point in a market, we can invest with confidence.

To make our entry signals safer, we must find entry points with a high success rate. This does not mean that every trade will be a winning trade. Getting stopped-out on stop-losses, and reentering a market while maintaining strict entry rules, stop-loss rules, and re-entry rules are all part of using Fibonacci trading devices in volatile markets.

When we are generating trading signals based on the final point of a PHI-ellipse, we sell high and buy low. This countertrend approach requires a lot of discipline, and one must simply believe in the power of the Fibonacci tools when a trading signal appears.

Four geometric Fibonacci trading devices have now been described and analyzed: (1) the Fibonacci summation series, (2) corrections and extensions, (3) PHI-channels, and (4) PHI-ellipses. Only two Fibonacci trading devices are still to come: PHI-spirals (Chapter 6) and Fibonacci time-goal analysis (Chapter 7). These will be explained separately, before all the tools are linked together in the final chapter.

6

PHI-Spirals

PHI-spirals end the long search for a way to forecast both time and price and to provide the link between price and time analysis. To relate nature's law to patterns of investor behavior expressed in the price swings of currencies, commodities, futures, or stocks, we must look to PHI-spirals. Any point on a spiral represents the optimal relationship of price and time.

The only mathematical curve that follows the pattern of natural growth is the spiral, expressed in natural phenomena such as the spira mirabilis—more commonly known as the nautilus shell. The key geometric features of spirals were presented in the first chapter. In this chapter, we will review some of their most striking characteristics.

In simple geometric terms, the size of a PHI-spiral is determined by the distance between the center (X) of the spiral and the starting point (A). The starting point is usually given by wave 1 or wave 2, which can be either a peak (in uptrends) or a valley (in downtrends). The corresponding center of the spiral is usually set to the beginning of the respective wave. The PHI-spiral then turns either clockwise or counterclockwise around the initial line that goes from the center to the starting point. As the PHI-spiral grows, it extends by a constant ratio with every full cycle.

Question 6–1:
How is the Fibonacci ratio PHI = 1.618 expressed in the PHI-spiral in Figure 6.1?

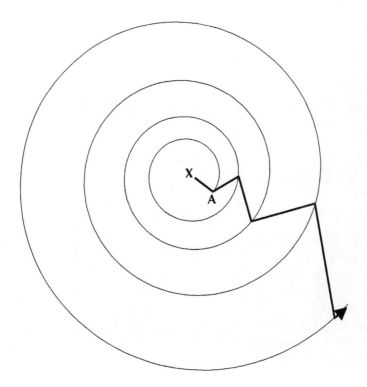

Figure 6.1   PHI-spiral. *Source:* FAM Research, 2000.

The most interesting feature of PHI-spirals is their development in extreme market situations, when investor behavior patterns are most evident.

The stock market crash in October 1987 is an example of a market situation that strongly illustrated investors' behavior. At a stage where most other methods of market analysis fail, the correct use of a PHI-spiral is able to pinpoint the bottom of a sharp market move.

The exactness of the PHI-spiral analysis captured the crash pattern of October 1987, as demonstrated in Figure 6.2, an example chart of the S&P500 Index.

With the center of the PHI-spiral at point X and the start at point A, the PHI-spiral is penetrated by the S&P500 Index at the lowest low: point P at the fourth spiral ring. The two points X and A are definitive and could have been selected by any investor (Figure 6.2).

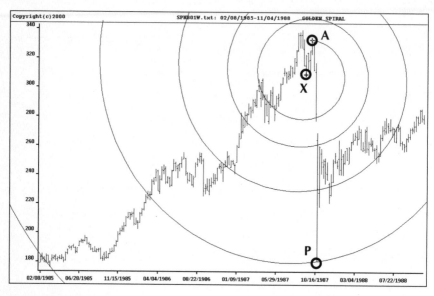

Figure 6.2   S&P500 Index from 02–85 to 11–88. The PHI-spiral pinpoints the low of the stock market crash in October 1987. *Source:* **FAM Research, 2000.**

BASIC FEATURES OF PHI-SPIRALS

As geometric Fibonacci trading devices, PHI-spirals are easy to understand and conceptually simple to apply to market price movements.

PHI-spirals identify trend reversals in the marketplace; therefore, trading signals based on PHI-spirals require investment action against the main trend. Valid countertrend investment decisions require exceptional discipline, accuracy in executing trading signals, and trust in the trading strategy.

Investing with PHI-spirals is neither a black-box approach nor an overfitted computerized trading system. It is, rather, a simple universal geometric law applied to different sorts of products, such as futures, stock index futures, stocks, or cash currencies.

Market Symmetry

PHI-spirals give evidence of a stunning symmetry in price patterns and show that price moves are not random. We regard symmetry in the markets as an expression of investors' behavior and nature's law.

Figure 6.3 illustrates a symmetrical downtrend price move in the Euro cash currency against the US Dollar.

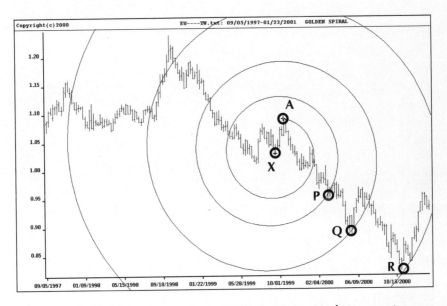

Figure 6.3   Euro cash currency from 09–97 to 01–01. Market symmetry captured by a PHI-spiral. *Source:* **FAM Research, 2000.**

Rule of Alternation

The rule of alternation goes hand in hand with the Fibonacci summation series and the Fibonacci ratios. It can be applied to price patterns in futures, cash currencies, and other products.

The rule of alternation in relation to PHI-spirals is best described by Jay Hambridge in the example of a sunflower: "In the sunflower, two sets of equiangular spirals are superimposed or intertwined, one being right-handed, and one a left-handed spiral, with each floret filling a dual role by belonging to both spirals."

Elliott knew about the rule of alternation. This rule made it possible for him to claim that he could forecast future price moves based on formations in wave 2 and wave 4 price patterns. (See Chapter 1 for a review of Elliott's wave principles.)

Exercise 6–A:

In the Crude Oil chart (Figure 6.4), what is the rationale behind the rule of alternation in relation to the PHI-spiral?

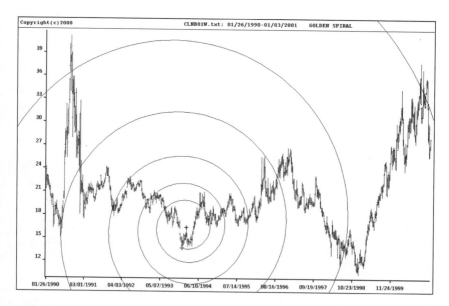

Figure 6.4   Crude oil from 01–90 to 01–01. *Source:* FAM Research, 2000.

Does the example of the rule of alternation in Figure 6.4 mean that the PHI-spirals are proficient forecasting instruments? Does it mean that the rule of alternation will tell us when there will be a high or low in the market? The answer to both questions is "Maybe." Although the rule of alternation is seen too often to be ignored, there is no guarantee that market prices will always conform.

Exercise 6–B:
Name the possible problems when using PHI-spiral rings to recognize the rule of alternation (Figure 6.5).

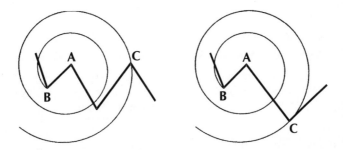

Figure 6.5   Identification of peaks and valleys based on PHI-spirals. *Source: Fibonacci Applications and Strategies for Traders,* R. Fischer (New York: Wiley, 1993), p. 138.

Name the key difference between the two PHI-spirals in Figure 6.6.

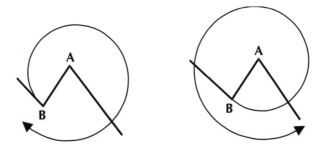

Figure 6.6   Rotation of PHI-spirals. *Source: Fibonacci Applications and Strategies for Traders,* R. Fischer (New York: Wiley, 1993), p. 140.

Swing Sizes

The swing size calculated from significant peaks and valleys determines the size of the PHI-spiral. A minimum swing size is required because a PHI-spiral has a minimum radius to properly rotate. Finding appropriate swing sizes on daily and weekly charts is mechanical and can be easily mastered.

To find the best swing sizes for a product, historical data and a constant scale are crucial. Every product has a special market behavior; therefore, swing sizes vary from product to product. As a guideline, some useful swing sizes for a variety of products are shown in Table 6.1.

Table 6.1   Sample Swing Sizes Daily and Weekly

Product	Daily Swing Size in Points	Daily Sample Move	Weekly Swing Size in Points
S&P500 Index	40.00	1,300.00 to 1,340.00	80.00
DAX30 Index	100.00	6,400.00 to 6,500.00	200.00
Crude Oil	2.00	20.00 to 22.00	4.00
Soybeans	20.00	520.00 to 540.00	40.00
Pork Bellies	2.00	50.00 to 52.00	4.00
Euro	0.02	0.92 to 0.94	0.04
Japanese Yen	2.00	110.00 to 112.00	4.00

Question 6–2:
Why is the swing size so important for analysis with PHI-spirals?

Specifications of PHI-Spirals

Finding the center and the appropriate starting point of a PHI-spiral is the most crucial part of the analysis. Almost every major turning point in the markets can be pinpointed if the correct PHI-spiral is chosen.

3-wave moves running in an a–b–c correction are the basic patterns we look for when setting up PHI-spirals. Patterns of this type include everything needed for reliable forecasting of market turning points.

The four different combinations of 3-wave patterns are shown in Figure 6.7.

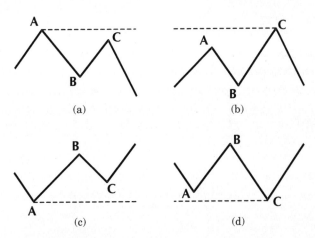

Figure 6.7   3-swing relations of A, B, and C. (a) Downtrend with high in A; (b) downtrend with high in C; (c) uptrend with low in A; (d) uptrend with low in C. *Source: Fibonacci Applications and Strategies for Traders,* **R. Fischer (New York: Wiley, 1993), p. 142.**

Whenever we use a 3-swing pattern, we have the option of locating the center of a PHI-spiral at point A, B, or C. Our research shows that the best results are achieved by using point B as the center for generating PHI-spirals; however, there is no fixed rule that the center of PHI-spirals must be set to point B. Points A and C may be valid, too.

In addition to the center point and the starting point of PHI-spirals, the clockwise or counterclockwise direction in which PHI-spirals are rotated is a decisive parameter.

Question 6–3:
Given all the possibilities, how do we know whether we have chosen a correct PHI-spiral?

Question 6–4:
Why do we require the third PHI-spiral ring of the PHI-spiral to be penetrated when we are looking for significant turning points?

Question 6–5:
Up to this point, we have been working with specific PHI-spirals and turning points. Is it possible for the same significant turning point to be identified simultaneously with several different PHI-spiral rings from different centers and different starting points?

WORKING WITH PHI-SPIRALS

For successful trading with PHI-spirals, we must identify which PHI-spirals are important and which are not. Whenever we look at a chart and try to find the next significant turning point of the market price, we realize that any peak or valley on the historical data might be the center or the starting point of an ideal PHI-spiral.

To solve this problem, we look for a crossover of at least two PHI-spiral rings that stem from two different PHI-spirals with different centers and starting points. The crossover should occur at the third (or a higher) PHI-spiral ring.

All these requirements sound very technical and complicated, but, in reality, they are very logical once the reader gets used to the WINPHI program and learns how to work with PHI-spirals.

In this chapter, we want to be a bit more specific about how to work with PHI-spirals.

For successful trading on PHI-spirals, we need at least two (or more) PHI-spirals identifying the same significant peak or valley in the stream of market data. These PHI-spirals can result from: (a) the selection of one and the same center and starting point, with PHI-spirals turned clockwise or counterclockwise; (b) different PHI-spirals with different centers and starting points; or (c) PHI-spirals on weekly and daily data.

Different PHI-spirals do not necessarily have to come from earlier and nearby swings. Significant peaks or valleys may also be discovered by PHI-spirals using swing formations weeks or months earlier.

When conducting a PHI-spiral analysis, the investor will not know which PHI-spirals are the correct ones at the beginning of a market move. Only future market action can tell. Therefore, it takes a lot of patience and discipline to wait for a crossover point of PHI-spirals and an indication that it is the appropriate time to invest.

Question 6–6:
Why is it better to look for the crossover points of *two* PHI-spirals than to work with just *one* PHI-spiral?

We do not present the PHI-spirals as stand-alone trading tools. This is done on purpose; the investor can easily integrate entry and exit signals (see Chapters 3 and 5), once a crossover point of two PHI-spirals is reached.

The more important question is: How can trading signals be made safer for investment? In this respect, the PHI-spiral is an excellent trading tool if combined with PHI-ellipses.

Question 6–7:
What is the biggest advantage of combining the analysis of PHI-spirals and PHI-ellipses into one trading tool?

Question 6–8:
Will the combination of the analysis based on PHI-spirals and PHI-ellipses *always* improve the quality of our trading signals?

ANSWERS TO QUESTIONS AND EXERCISES

In Chapter 6, we have introduced how to work with PHI-spirals. These concepts are described in more detail in *The New Fibonacci Trader,* pages 195–258.

In this workbook, we concentrate on how to identify the basic structure of the PHI-spiral and how to integrate other Fibonacci trading devices. All of the exercises can be reproduced using the WINPHI program and the historical data on the CD-ROM provided with the textbook. Readers who want a real-time update of the data can go to our online version of the WINPHI software, on a registered membership basis, at **www.fibotrader.com.**

Answer to Question 6–1:

PHI-spirals are perfect geometric approximations of nature's law and natural growth. As the PHI-spiral grows, it increases by a constant ratio 1.618 with every full cycle (Figure 6.8).

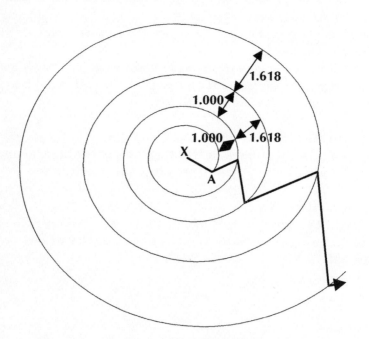

Figure 6.8   PHI-spiral. *Source:* FAM Research, 2000.

Exercise 6–A:

The rule of alternation means that after a peak comes a valley, then another peak followed by another valley, and so on. This same principle is seen in nature, as demonstrated in the sunflower (see Chapter 1).

In the Crude Oil chart (Figure 6.9), we see the same principle.

The center of the PHI-spiral is at point X, its starting point is at the valley in A, and it is rotated counterclockwise. The first peak is reached at point P on the second PHI-spiral ring. The valley that follows is marked when the third PHI-spiral ring, at point Q, is penetrated.

The valley is followed by a peak at point R, once the fourth PHI-spiral ring is penetrated. The peak alternates with a new valley at point S, on the fifth PHI-spiral ring. The valley alternates with another peak at point T when the sixth PHI-spiral ring is penetrated.

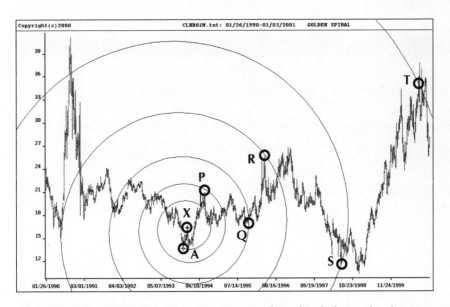

Figure 6.9 Crude Oil from 01–90 to 01–01. The rule of alternation is represented by a PHI-spiral. *Source:* FAM Research, 2000.

Exercise 6–B:

Although the rule of alternation is often seen, its particular pattern may differ. Once the market price touches a PHI-spiral ring with a low point, it will not necessarily go higher to touch the next PHI-spiral ring with a high. Instead, it may keep going lower. These two possibilities are shown in Figure 6.10.

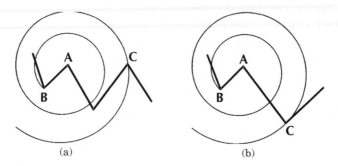

Figure 6.10 Identification of peaks and valleys based on PHI-spirals. (a) Definition of a new high; (b) definition of a new low. *Source: Fibonacci Applications and Strategies for Traders,* R. Fischer (New York: Wiley, 1993), p. 138.

Adding to the uncertainty as to whether a new high or low is defined when a PHI-spiral ring is penetrated, PHI-spirals can turn either counterclockwise or clockwise, beginning with the same center and starting point. The two directions of rotation are presented in Figure 6.11.

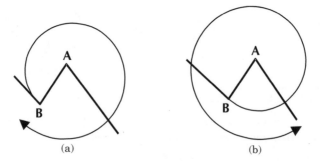

Figure 6.11 PHI-spiral rotation. (a) Clockwise; (b) counterclockwise. *Source: Fibonacci Applications and Strategies for Traders,* R. Fischer (New York: Wiley, 1993), p. 140.

Answer to Question 6–2:

If the swing size is too small, there will be a lot of noise in the market, making PHI-spirals unreliable. If the swing size is too large, the PHI-spiral rings are too far away from each other and are of no value to the analysis.

Answer to Question 6–3:

Whenever we work with PHI-spirals in price analysis, there will be one PHI-spiral that is stable, and another that precisely identifies the rhythm of a market pattern. To find this special PHI-spiral, we must always start our analysis with the center of the PHI-spiral—point B. The starting point of the PHI-spiral can be either point A or point C.

A PHI-spiral that identifies a market price pattern catches the first or second significant turning point and then goes on to identify other turning points. This is shown in Figure 6.12 for the DAX30 Index.

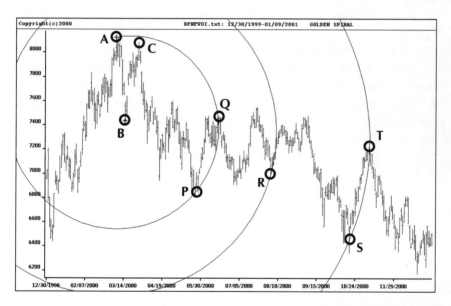

Figure 6.12 DAX30 Index from 12–99 to 01–01. The PHI-spiral rotated clockwise. The center is at point B and the starting point is at A. *Source:* FAM Research, 2000.

Answer to Question 6–4:

Whenever we are working with PHI-spirals—on weekly, daily, or intraday charts—we need to be far enough away from the starting point of the PHI-spiral.

PHI-spiral analysis always works against the main trend direction, so we need enough distance between the initial starting point of the PHI-spiral and the point where the PHI-spiral ring is touched to have room for a market retracement to make money.

In other words: If we use the first PHI-spiral ring for the analysis, the distance between the starting point of the PHI-spiral and the point where the first PHI-spiral ring is touched might be 30 basis points in the S&P500 Index (a sample price movement from 1,200.00 to 1,230.00). But if we wait until the third PHI-spiral ring is touched, the distance might be 100 basis points or more. In this case, there is a much better chance to make money if the market price corrects and reverses its direction, because we are investing countertrend.

Working with the third PHI-spiral ring is also important because we can eliminate the noise from smaller swings that might have been touched by the first or second PHI-spiral ring.

Answer to Question 6–5:

Part of the strength of PHI-spirals comes from their identification of significant turning points in the markets far in advance, with different PHI-spirals starting from different peaks or valleys, and with different centers.

In Figure 6.13, we show eight different PHI-spirals pinpointing the highest high of the S&P500 Index months—or even years—ahead of time. All eight PHI-spirals differ in their starting point, center, and/or direction of rotation.

Usually, price and time targets on third PHI-spiral rings in the markets are so far away from the current trading action that they cannot be trusted; we never know whether these targets will ever be reached. But at the point where the targets in time and price are reached, no one looks back far enough in the analysis.

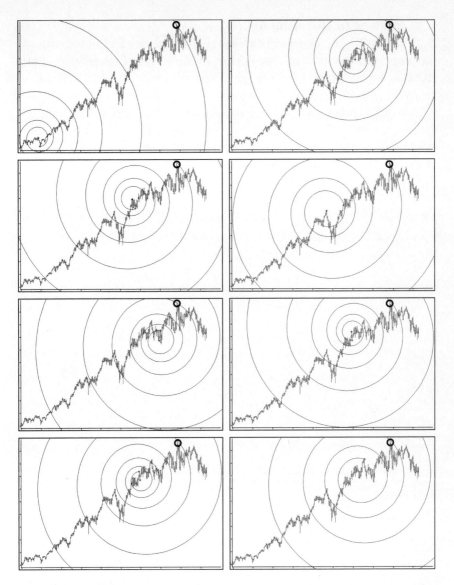

Figure 6.13   S&P500 Index from 01–96 to 01–01. Multiple PHI-spiral confirmations of the all-time high. *Source:* FAM Research, 2000.

Answer to Question 6–6:

The following elements can cause uncertainty in the selection of the correct PHI-spiral: (a) swing size; (b) direction of rotation; (c) PHI-spiral starting point; (d) PHI-spiral center; (e) number of PHI-spiral rings.

To eliminate uncertainty in selecting the correct PHI-spirals, we look for those that have a crossover point at least at the third PHI-spiral ring when the market price reaches the crossover point. This is shown in the example of the DAX30 Index (Figure 6.14).

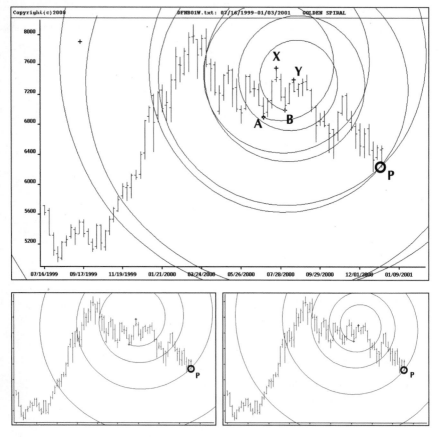

Figure 6.14   DAX30 Index from 07–99 to 01–01. *Source:* **FAM Research, 2000.**

Regardless of how we get crossovers of PHI-spirals—whether from the changing of rotation, or from varying central points or starting points—the crossover of PHI-spirals reveals the potential turning points in major markets.

In the DAX30 Index, both PHI-spirals have centers at points A and B. The starting points are at X and Y. The first PHI-spiral turns clockwise; the second one turns counterclockwise. The crossover of the two PHI-spirals happens at the significant valley point P where both PHI-spirals have their third PHI-spiral rings.

The problem with applying only one PHI-spiral to a chart is that there is no way of knowing, from the many possible PHI-spirals, which one would be the most stable and, therefore, the best to correctly identify significant peaks. This is why we now look primarily for crossovers of PHI-spirals as confirmations of significant trend reversals. The strategy of looking for crossover points in PHI-spirals can be applied to weekly, daily, or intraday data.

When we start the PHI-spirals, we do not know whether the crossover point in the third PHI-spiral ring will ever be reached by the market price. We must always wait to see what the market's price pattern is doing, and that picture will unfold over a period of time.

Answer to Question 6–7:

Combining PHI-ellipses and PHI-spirals is a highly effective strategy because the confirmation of two Fibonacci trading tools makes it much easier to find a significant turning point in a price move.

When we start with the PHI-ellipse, we know exactly where we are in a price move, for we need at least a 3-wave pattern, and the third wave must be longer than the first impulse wave to eliminate the noise in sideward markets. By integrating the slope of the PHI-ellipse, we will buy low or sell high. This does not mean that we will always sell at the highest high or buy at the lowest low, but our buy-sell pattern will be quite repetitive.

Figure 6.15 shows a sample chart for the Euro cash currency between April and November 2000, to demonstrate how fruitful the combination of PHI-spirals and PHI-ellipses can be.

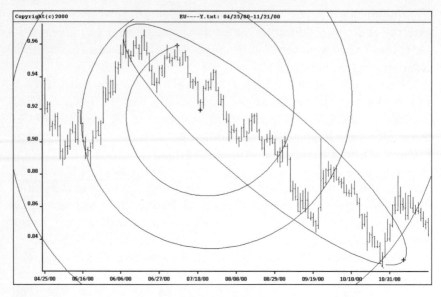

Figure 6.15   Euro cash currency from 04–00 to 11–00. PHI-spiral and PHI-ellipse combined. *Source:* FAM Research, 2000.

Answer to Question 6–8:

In Chapter 5, we showed how the quality of the PHI-ellipse depended on the designated 3-wave pattern. Although the price patterns are available for the PHI-ellipse in most cases, there are times, in extreme market moves up or down, when the 3-wave pattern does not appear and thus the PHI-ellipse cannot be used.

In Figure 6.16, we show an example of such an exceptional situation, using weekly data of the Deutsche Bank stock.

In 1998, the stock price collapsed from about 80 DEM to 40 DEM in 10 weeks, so there were no swings on the weekly data. Note, however, that the significant low was perfectly pinpointed with the crossover of two PHI-spirals.

We show this chart to demonstrate that there are always exceptions to the rule. Should we be in a strong, extended market move with no swings, we can use the crossover point of the PHI-spirals, instead of the PHI-ellipse, to make our investment decision.

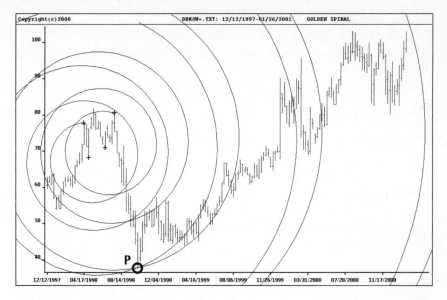

Figure 6.16   Deutsche Bank stock from 12–97 to 01–01. Crossover of PHI-spirals. *Source:* FAM Research, 2000.

FINAL REMARKS

PHI-spirals provide the missing analytical link between geometric price and time analysis. PHI-spirals, considered the most beautiful of all mathematical curves, have occurred in nature for millions of years. To link nature's law to human behavior expressed in the price swings of financial futures, stock index futures, stocks, and cash currencies, we must look to the PHI-spiral.

PHI-spirals prove that market price patterns are not random, for there is a stunning symmetry in each major product traded. Each product follows a clear behavioral pattern. The forces that direct price moves also allow investors to take advantage of trading opportunities, as long as investors are capable of correctly applying PHI-spirals.

PHI-spirals are simple to work with and easy to understand; just one center and one starting point must be chosen per PHI-spiral. However, PHI-spirals cannot be drawn by hand. A software package like our WINPHI computer program is needed to chart them.

The main challenge in PHI-spiral analysis is actually rather simple: Just believe in it. Crossover points of PHI-spirals occur at extreme points in the markets and are always countertrends to the main trend direction. Discipline and patience are crucial.

Looking for crossover points while working with PHI-spirals eliminates the uncertainty that might emerge when choosing the starting point or the center of a PHI-spiral. We need at least three PHI-spiral rings to get a valid signal, which then filters out the noise created by many smaller swings.

A combination of PHI-spirals and PHI-ellipses is a highly recommended trading strategy. By combining the strength of the PHI-ellipses and PHI-spirals, trading signals become more reliable in any product or data form.

7

FIBONACCI TIME-
GOAL ANALYSIS

In 1983, in the United States, Robert Fischer presented a series of seminars that introduced the ways in which the Fibonacci ratio could be productively applied to time-goal days (TGDs).

The Fibonacci time-goal analysis is similar to the time analysis based on the Fibonacci summation series (see Chapter 2), but instead of using the Fibonacci summation series to forecast turning points in the markets, Fibonacci time-goal analysis uses the Fibonacci ratios 0.618, 1.000, and 1.618. Time-goal days can also be confirmed by higher ratios from the PHI series, but the examples herein will concentrate on these three fundamental ratios because they stem directly from the Fibonacci summation series.

Fibonacci time-goal days are days on which a price event is supposed to occur. Being able to anticipate the exact day on which a price trend might change direction is helpful in our daily and weekly analyses, and corresponds to the analysis we performed with PHI-ellipses and PHI-spirals. Fibonacci time-goal analysis is not lagging; it has forecasting value. Trades can be entered or exited *at* the price change rather than after the fact. The concept is dynamic. The distance between two highs or two lows is seldom the same, and precalculated Fibonacci time-goal days vary, depending on larger or smaller swing sizes of a market pattern.

To properly calculate Fibonacci time-goal days, we draw upon the work of the Greek mathematician, Euclid of Megara, and his invention of the golden cut (also called the golden section), which links nature's law to geometry. (For a review of this concept and how it relates to trading, see Chapter 1.)

In accordance with Euclid's findings, we take the distance between two peaks or two valleys as the basis for calculating Fibonacci time-goal days. The distance from peak to peak or from valley to valley is multiplied by the ratio 1.618, which identifies a point in the future where the major trend reversal can be expected. (See Figure 7.1 for a peak-to-peak formation.)

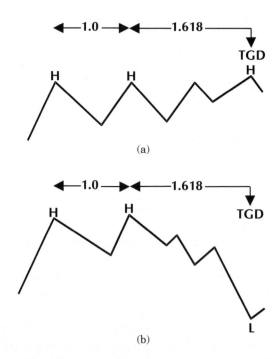

Figure 7.1 Fibonacci time-goal days. (a) Market price is high on a time-goal day out of a peak-to-peak formation; (b) market price is low on a time-goal day out of a peak-to-peak formation. *Source:* FAM Research, 2000.

Fibonacci time-goal days can be measured on weekly, daily, or intraday data series using the ratios 0.618, 1.000, or 1.618, but, as we will see later, the ratio 1.618 is considered the standard and is used most often.

In the following exercises and questions, we will introduce the basic principles of the Fibonacci time-goal analysis. Readers will find that the ratios and rules are the same as those discussed in previous chapters, but are used differently.

SOME BASICS ON FIBONACCI TIME-GOAL DAYS

Fibonacci time-goal analysis forecasts changes in trend direction. Therefore, traders must be prepared to buy when the price is low and sell when the price is high.

This strategy may sound simple, but it is difficult to execute because emotion usually drives traders to buy strongly on uptrends, in expectation of further rising prices, and to sell on downtrends, in expectation of lower lows.

Question 7–1:
Will the market price be high or low when the Fibonacci time-goal day is reached?

Question 7–2:
Are the trading signals generated with Fibonacci time-goal days in the direction of the main trend or a countertrend?

Swing Sizes

The key parameter for calculating TGDs is the size of the initial swing that defines the valid peaks and valleys.

Each product we analyze has a particular minimum swing size. Swing sizes vary, depending on the product and the chosen data compression rate (monthly, weekly, daily, or intraday).

In our analysis, we work strictly with the sequence high/high and low/low, in order to be able to create a time band. We see combinations of high/low or low/high on weekly charts when not enough swings are available.

We will always work with an entry rule, an exit rule, and a stop-loss rule because we believe in risk control. These rules have already been described in Chapter 3. They are reliable and can be safely combined with TGDs.

Question 7–3:
How does the swing size affect our analysis, and thus, our trading?

No matter how closely we look for the best minimum swing size, there will be situations, especially in strong trending markets, in which the minimum swing size is not available. "Not available," in this case, means that we will not find valid swing highs or swing lows in a market move over a long period of time, even though there will be many smaller price swings.

As a general rule, valid swing highs and valid swing lows must occur at least every 15 days on daily data, or every 10 weeks on weekly data. If swing highs and lows occur less frequently, the Fibonacci time-goal days will be so far apart that trend reversals can no longer be captured. Reducing the swing size below its optimal level solves this problem. We simply select the highest peaks or the lowest valley of 15 days or 10 weeks, and then designate a new measurement for a valid swing to calculate a Fibonacci time goal.

Question 7–4:
What do we do if there are too many swing highs or lows and we do not know which one to use?

Applications of Fibonacci time-goal days do not require the use of a wave count. In Fibonacci time analysis, it is not important to have a particular (uptrend, downtrend, or sideways) market. The Fibonacci ratios can be applied to any predefined market swing pattern.

Fibonacci time-goal days forecast events in time. We never know whether a market price will be high or low by the time a Fibonacci time-goal day is reached. Our primary objective is to sell on the time-goal day if the market price is high, and to buy on the time-goal day if the market price is low.

Confirmations

In our analyses, the multiple confirmation of a trend reversal provides the most solid basis for investment decisions. Multiple confirmations are also very important to our Fibonacci time analysis.

Market entries in Fibonacci time analysis are based on double confirmations of time-goal days. A trend reversal must be confirmed by one Fibonacci time-goal day that is calculated from two peaks (or valleys) and a second Fibonacci time-goal day that is calculated from two valleys (or peaks).

Figure 7.2 illustrates the main rule for confirming Fibonacci time-goal days.

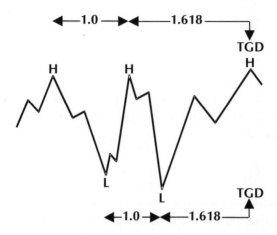

Figure 7.2 Fibonacci time-goal days coinside based on a peak-to-peak and a valley-to-valley formation. *Source:* FAM Research, 2000.

The perfect case occurs when one Fibonacci time goal calculated from two peaks, and another Fibonacci goal calculated from two valleys, point at exactly the same day.

Having a pair of Fibonacci time goals is an exception to the rule that Fibonacci time-goal days must be interspersed. To receive the multiple confirmation of a trend reversal, Fibonacci time-goal days must be close together; the precalculated time goal must not differ for more than two days or two weeks. If this does *not* happen, we do not act at all; we must wait until two Fibonacci time goals are again confirmed close enough together.

In most cases, the first Fibonacci time goal points to one day or one week shortly before a peak or valley. The second Fibonacci time goal often points right at the peak or valley. We receive a narrow time band of a few days for the appearance of a trend reversal. (This time band is similar to the price bands described for corrections and extensions in Chapter 3.)

Whenever a Fibonacci time goal points three or more days—or three or more weeks—after a peak or valley, it can be ignored, as long as we do not find another possible minimum filter swing from which to calculate.

The basic features of Fibonacci time goals are easy to understand and are not difficult to apply to market data on a daily or weekly basis.

WORKING WITH FIBONACCI TIME-GOAL DAYS

In the previous chapters on PHI-ellipses and PHI-spirals, we showed how weekly analysis and daily analysis complement each other and must be considered together if we are to have a clear overall picture of the market strategy.

The advantage of using weekly data is that many of the smaller swings are eliminated, and we can concentrate our analysis on major trend changes. This does not mean, however, that trend changes analyzed with daily data have no value.

Daily trend changes are of great importance for investors who focus on smaller short-term swings and who trade more frequently. Trend changes on daily data are also very important for intraday traders seeking confirmations of their intraday signals.

S&P500 Index Weekly

We will first analyze the S&P500 Index weekly data, and will look for confirmations of trend reversals where Fibonacci time-goal days are not more than two weeks apart.

All weekly Fibonacci time goals in the S&P500 Index are calculated exclusively, based on high/high formations and/or low/low connections.

Exercise 7–A:
To learn how to work with the Fibonacci time-goal days, complete the following two steps:

(a) **Mark the significant peaks and valleys in Figure 7.3, using a minimum swing size of 80 basis points. If there is no minimum swing size for 10 weeks, the next smaller swing size is used. A peak or valley is confirmed when** there are two lower highs on either side of a high (or, for a low, two higher lows). A swing peak and valley can be on the same weekly price bar.

(b) After the significant highs and lows are identified, calculate the TGDs with the Fibonacci ratios 0.618, 1.000, and 1.618, and identify the trend changes.

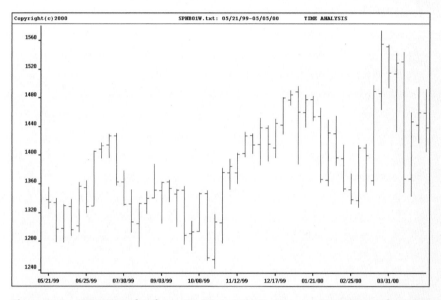

Figure 7.3   S&P500 Index from 05–99 to 05–00. *Source:* FAM Research, 2000.

S&P500 Index Daily

Fibonacci time-goal days occur much more frequently on daily data than on weekly data. If we limit the analysis to the ratio 1.618 for the first Fibonacci time-goal day and then use all three ratios—0.618, 1.000, and 1.618—to confirm the Fibonacci time-goal days, we can identify every major trend reversal daily, while staying very close to the market action.

The time band between the two Fibonacci time-goal days must not be wider than two days. This important rule will filter out irrelevant time targets.

Exercise 7–B gives the reader a chance to create Fibonacci time-goal days on daily data.

Exercise 7–B:
Complete the following two steps on the S&P500 Index:

(a) **In Figure 7.4, mark the significant swing highs and swing lows by using a minimum swing size of 45 basis points.**

(b) **Once the significant highs and lows are identified, find the significant trend changes by using the most important Fibonacci ratio, 1.618.**

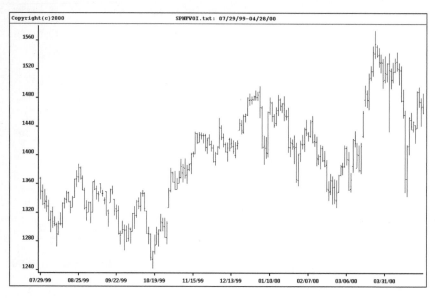

Figure 7.4   S&P500 Index from 07–99 to 04–00.

ANSWERS TO QUESTIONS AND EXERCISES

In Chapter 7, we have introduced Fibonacci time-goal days as trading devices. Although this workbook gives a basic overview on how to properly work with this trading tool, *The New Fibonacci Trader* contains full and detailed explanations (see pages 259–276), and each example can be reproduced with the WINPHI program and its historical data.

Shortly after this book is available, there will be a significant time gap between the published charts and real-time trading. Therefore, interested readers should visit the online version of the WINPHI software package, at **www.fibotrader.com,** on a registered membership basis.

Answer to Question 7–1:

As we can conclude from the price moves in Figure 7.1, the market price can be either high or low when the TGD is reached.

Answer to Question 7–2:

All trading signals we generate with TGDs are countertrend, which means that if the market price is high when a TGD is reached, we sell, and when the market price at a Fibonacci time goal is low, we buy.

Answer to Question 7–3:

The number of trades is (negatively) correlated with the swing size because if the swing size is too small, there will be too many Fibonacci time-goal days and too many potential trend changes. If the swing size is too large, there will be very few signals and important price moves are likely to be missed.

Answer to Question 7–4:

A reformulation of the swing definition is necessary when there is a strongly increased number of swing highs or lows in only a few days or a few weeks. Too high a frequency of swing highs or swing lows means increased noise in the market, and this can be a major problem in volatile market conditions.

Excessive noise can be eliminated by a simple amendment to the general definition of filter swings. There must be at least three days (or weeks) between the highs and lows of two swings that satisfy a minimum swing size. This applies to both top and bottom formations.

Exercise 7–A:

To create Fibonacci time-goal days, all we need is the minimum swing size, to identify the significant peaks and valleys, and the Fibonacci ratios 0.618, 1.000, and 1.618, to create time bands. We can designate a smaller minimum swing size when the weekly price pattern does not show a minimum swing size for more than 10 weeks.

We marked the significant peaks and valleys from #1 to #16 in Figure 7.5. Peak #8 and valley #9 have a smaller minimum swing size but are necessary because there was no minimum swing price pattern available for 10 weeks. Table 7.1 lists the characteristics of the peaks and valleys.

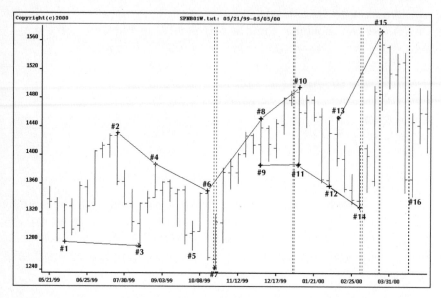

Figure 7.5   S&P500 Index from 05–99 to 05–00. *Source:* FAM Research, 2000.

Table 7.1   Characteristics of Peaks and Valleys

Turning Point	Type	High#/Low# Reference	Ratio
#7	Valley	H#2/H#4	1.618
		L#1/L#3	0.618
#10	Peak	H#4/H#6	1.618
		L#9/L#11	0.618
#14	Valley	L#9/L#11	1.618
		H#8/H#10	1.618
#15	Peak	H#10/H#13	1.618
		L#11/L#12	1.618
#16	Valley	L#12/L#14	1.618
		H#13/H#15	0.618

Exercise 7–B:

On the daily chart of the S&P500 Index (Figure 7.6), we created the Fibonacci time-goal days by using the ratio 1.618. We have 10 trend changes and we have analyzed 27 significant peaks and valleys (see Table 7.2). The peak #X and the valley #Y are integrated, for there was no significant minimum swing size between valley #9 and peak #10 in 15 days. To make analysis easier for the reader, we did not include time bands, but the same chart, with the time bands, is shown in Figure 7.7.

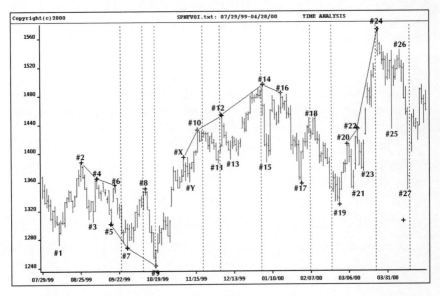

Figure 7.6 S&P500 Index from 07–99 to 04–00. *Source:* FAM Research, 2000.

Table 7.2 Characteristics of Significant Peaks and Valleys

Turning Point	Type	High#/Low# Reference	Ratio
#7	Valley	H#2/H#4	1.618
#8	Peak	H#4/H#6	1.618
#9	Valley	L#5/L#7	1.618
#10	Peak	L#7/L#9	1.618
#11	Valley	H#X/H#10	1.618
#14	Peak	H#10/H#12	1.618
#18	Peak	H#14/H#18	1.618
#19	Valley	H#12/H#14	1.618
#24	Peak	H#20/H#22	1.618
#27	Valley	H#22/H#24	1.618

Analyzing trend changes with Fibonacci time goals illustrates the power of this investment tool. It is very important to understand that these particular trend changes are created by using the Fibonacci ratio 1.618, but we can also use calculations from the three ratios— 0.618, 1.000, or 1.618—for confirmation and to create time bands (see Figure 7.7).

From valley #9 to peak #10, there was no valid minimum swing size. Because more than 15 days passed between the peak and the valley, we used the next smaller swing size, marked #X for the peak and #Y for the valley.

On peak #14 and peak #18, we found two significant trend changes; both were peaks without a valley in between. In such a case, the trader must leave the stop-loss order in the market until a new significant valley is identified with Fibonacci time-goal analysis.

Figure 7.7 shows what the daily S&P500 Index looks like when the time band is created with the standard ratio 1.618, and with another ratio (0.618, 1.000, or 1.618) for confirmation.

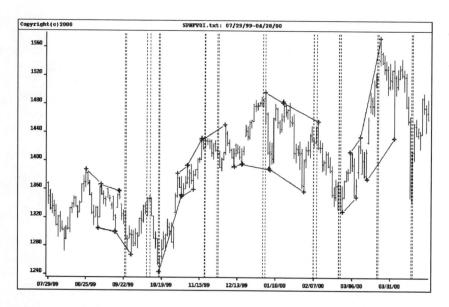

Figure 7.7 S&P500 Index from 07–99 to 04–00 (time bands added). *Source:* FAM Research, 2000.

FINAL REMARKS

Fibonacci time-goal analysis is similar to the time analysis based on the Fibonacci summation series, as described in Chapter 2. However, instead of using the numbers of the Fibonacci summation series to forecast trend reversals, Fibonacci time-goal days are calculated from swing highs and swing lows. Ratio 1.618 is used as the standard, and ratios 0.618, 1.000, and 1.618 are used for confirmations and to create the time bands.

In this chapter, we did not explain how to integrate entry and exit rules, for they have already been explained in Chapter 3, along with extensions and corrections.

Fibonacci time-goal days can be applied to monthly, weekly, daily, or intraday charts. The more Fibonacci time-goal days that point to the same trend reversal, the greater the chances that a trend reversal will occur at the precalculated target.

Successful Fibonacci time analysis depends on the correct identification of peaks and valleys. To find the most consistent (standard) swing sizes for every product, the reader should have access to the historical data and the charting features of the WINPHI software, provided with *The New Fibonacci Trader*. These datasets can be used to find appropriate minimum swings for the major products in the market. The WINPHI charting feature works with ASCII D–O–H–L–C data, so that files from any major data vendor can be loaded into the program after being converted to plain ASCII format.

8

WORKING WITH
FIBONACCI TRADING TOOLS:
TWO STRATEGIES

Can the trading strategies based on our six Fibonacci devices be improved by combining them? Can Fibonacci trading minimize risk and generate more profits? These are the key questions we will tackle in this chapter. To reach this goal, we will not continue to challenge the reader's knowledge with questions and exercises, but will focus on two strategies that are the basic structure when we want to apply the Fibonacci trading tools successfully.

Timing is the most crucial element in trading. It is important to know what to buy, but it is even more important to know *when* to buy. The best buy signals and profitable trades can result in losses if the investor does not know when to sell. In Chapters 2 through 7, we showed how each Fibonacci tool is able to serve investors as a profitable stand-alone trading solution in its own right. All trading signals result from the geometric interpretations of market price patterns. All six Fibonacci trading devices are based on the understanding of investor behavior as expressed in peak and valley formations.

Our most important discovery was that more than one of the Fibonacci tools could forecast trend changes at the same point in price and time. This is a unique finding and has never before been presented. This type of forecasting does not mean we will know whether a turning point is going to be triggered, but if a precalculated price target is reached, we can safely invest by following the rules given for the different geometric Fibonacci trading devices.

The basic application of geometric Fibonacci trading tools requires nothing more than the use of swing highs, swing lows, and the Fibonacci ratios. The biggest difficulty is choosing the *correct* swing highs or lows. On weekly price data, we cannot always apply all of the Fibonacci trading tools, because there are not always enough swings from which to calculate turning points. On daily data, we have a sufficient number of swing highs and swing lows, but we might get too many signals. An even higher number of trading signals is found on intraday data.

To solve this problem, we recommend looking for a trend change on weekly data when generating trades with daily data, and looking for a trend change on daily data when generating trades with intraday data.

STRATEGY A: COMBINING PHI-ELLIPSES WITH OTHER FIBONACCI TOOLS TO TRADE IN THE MAIN TREND DIRECTION

PHI-Ellipses and Corrections

In Chapters 3 and 5, we explained how to work with corrections and PHI-ellipses as separate Fibonacci trading tools. Now we will show how to combine them. The main idea behind this strategy is that, in many cases, we can expect a 3-wave price pattern, where wave 3, or the second impulse wave, is longer than wave 1, the first impulse wave. (See Figure 5.2 for a review.)

If we base our investments on the rules of corrections, we can draw a PHI-ellipse around the price pattern as soon as the market price moves above or below the peak or valley from wave 1. In these cases, PHI-ellipses can be used as stop-loss levels as well as profit targets. As long as the market price stays within the borders of the PHI-ellipse, the investor should stay invested, but once the market price moves out of the sidelines of the PHI-ellipse, trading action must be taken.

It is very important to understand that the first PHI-ellipse placed around the 3-wave pattern will never be the final one. The market price pattern develops over time, and the PHI-ellipse must be adjusted. As long as the correction is regular, points B and C will remain side points of the PHI-ellipse. Should we encounter an irregular correction, we will have a new side point C1 for the PHI-ellipse (Figure 8.1).

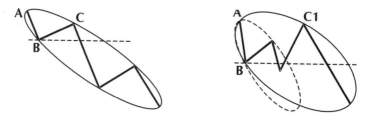

Figure 8.1   Adjustment of PHI-ellipses based on the duration of corrections.
Source: **FAM Research, 2000.**

The length of the PHI-ellipse might also have to be adjusted if the market price stays within the PHI-ellipse. The PHI-ellipse can become longer or shorter, thicker or thinner. Any adjustment can be done very easily with the WINPHI program.

PHI-Channel Line as Trailing Stop

When the first PHI-ellipse has been drawn, we can also draw the parallel to the baseline of the PHI-channel through the outside point of the PHI-channel at point C of the correction. This PHI-channel line can be used as a trailing stop.

In the chart of the Japanese Yen cash currency (Figure 8.2), entry signals are based on a three days' high or low, which also confirms point C as a significant high or low. The exit rule is based on the penetration of the PHI-channel line. Readers must remember that these signals are only for demonstration purposes because the time span is too short to be reliable. Longer test runs on historical data can be executed with the WINPHI software.

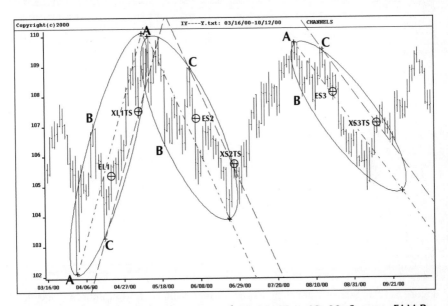

Figure 8.2   Japanese Yen cash currency from 03–00 to 10–00. *Source:* FAM Research, 2000. (Disclaimer: Past performance may not be indicative of future results.)

Fibonacci Trading Tools as Multiple Profit Targets

Although a PHI-ellipse can be established with the starting point and the side points, the final shape can change. The PHI-ellipse might be thicker or thinner, longer or shorter. To precalculate the final shape of the PHI-ellipse and determine the profit targets, we must integrate other Fibonacci trading tools.

The market price will not always reach this precalculated crossover point of different Fibonacci trading tools, but when it is reached (many times, it will be), we have a well-defined profit target.

The chart of the Japanese Yen cash currency (Figure 8.3) contains a correction, a PHI-ellipse, a PHI-spiral, an extension, and a

Fibonacci time-goal day, illustrating the use of multiple Fibonacci tools to define profit targets.

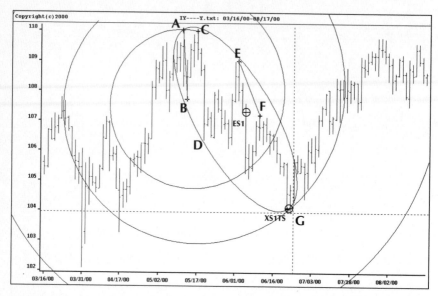

Figure 8.3   Japanese Yen cash currency from 03–00 to 08–00. *Source:* FAM Research, 2000. (Disclaimer: Past performance may not be indicative of future results.)

The five Fibonacci trading tools in Figure 8.3 should be combined, step-by-step, in the following order:

1. Correction (see Chapter 3)
   We must wait until the correction level of 61.8% is reached at the peak at point E, and then sell at a three days' low as an entry rule.

2. PHI-ellipse (see Chapter 5)
   Once market pricing goes below point D, the PHI-ellipse is drawn with the starting point at A and the two side points at D and E.

3. PHI-spiral (see Chapter 6)
   The PHI-spiral is drawn with a center at B and a starting point at C. In general, we look for the third PHI-spiral ring to determine the end of the PHI-ellipse, but if the initial swing size is big, we work with the second PHI-spiral ring. In this case, the second PHI-spiral ring confirms the end of the PHI-ellipse long before the market price reaches this point. If the initial swing size is small, we look for the fourth PHI-spiral ring.

4. Extension (see Chapter 3)
   Price goals with extensions are calculated by the distance from A to B, and multiplied by the Fibonacci ratio 1.618. The price goal reaches the end of the PHI-ellipse at point G, so we know that the end of the PHI-ellipse might also be at this point.

5. Fibonacci time-goal day (see Chapter 7)
   The Fibonacci time-goal day is calculated when the distance between peaks E and F is multiplied by the Fibonacci ratio 1.618. The Fibonacci time-goal day meets point G.

Therefore, when the market price reaches the profit target at point G, positions should be closed.

STRATEGY B: PHI-ELLIPSES COMBINED WITH OTHER FIBONACCI TOOLS TO TRADE COUNTER TO THE MAIN TREND

Daily Analysis of the DAX30 Index

Turning Points and PHI-Ellipses
In any analysis using PHI-ellipses, smaller PHI-ellipses can typically be part of a bigger 3-wave price pattern. Many times, a bigger PHI-ellipse surrounds three smaller PHI-ellipses, as seen in Figure 8.4, a sample DAX30 Index chart from June 2000 to June 2001.

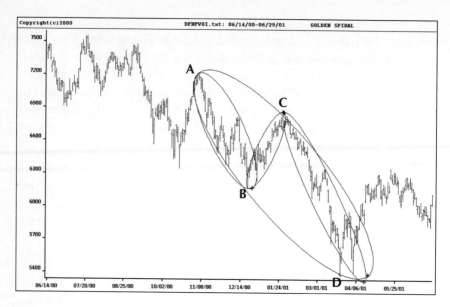

Figure 8.4   DAX30 Index from 06–00 to 06–01. *Source:* FAM Research, 2000.

The longer the market price movement stays within the PHI-ellipse, the more significant the turning points are when the market price reaches the very end of the PHI-ellipse. This is why we recommend looking for major trend changes on a daily basis, even when we execute trades based on intraday analysis.

The geometric Fibonacci tools are important because they can be used equally well on weekly, daily, or intraday data. The only difference is that, depending on the data compression rate, Fibonacci tools can be *applied* differently. Consequently, because there are more swings on hourly or 15-minute intraday data, we might be able to work with PHI-spirals that cannot be applied to daily data, for we do not have the same swing sizes available there. More detailed information on the use of PHI-spirals can be found in Chapter 6.

Turning Points and Multiple Fibonacci Tools

In addition to PHI-ellipses, turning points in the DAX30 Index can be identified by using a combination of PHI-spiral, extension, PHI-channel, and a Fibonacci time-goal day.

Price moves are analyzed through the basic structure of the PHI-ellipse. The end of the PHI-ellipse is multiply confirmed by integrating other Fibonacci trading tools (Figure 8.5).

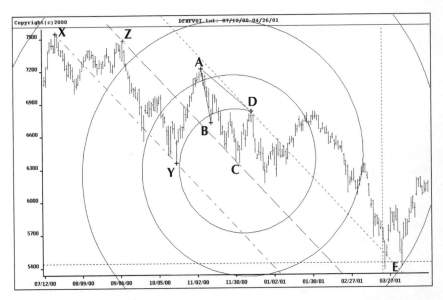

Figure 8.5   DAX30 Index from 07–00 to 04–01. *Source:* **FAM Research, 2000.**

All four geometric Fibonacci trading tools can be added to the chart, one after the other.

1. PHI-spiral (see Chapter 6)
   The PHI-spiral has its center at point C and its starting point at the peak at point D. The third PHI-spiral ring, turning counter-clockwise, confirms the end of the PHI-ellipse at point E. (We do not show the second PHI-spiral that creates the crossover point at point E.)

2. Extension (see Chapter 3)
   The price goal with extension is calculated when we multiply the distance from point A to point B by the Fibonacci ratio 1.618. The price target is almost identical to the lowest low of the market at point E.

3. PHI-channel (see Chapter 4)

   The PHI-channel has its baseline from X to Y and its outside point at Z. The width of the PHI-channel, multiplied by the ratio 1.000, generates the PHI-channel line, which also confirms the market bottom at point E.

4. Fibonacci time-goal day (see Chapter 7)

   When we multiply the distance from point A to point D by the ratio 1.618, we also identify the low of the market price using the Fibonacci time-goal day analysis.

Daily Analysis of the S&P500 Index

The S&P500 Index is the most watched stock index future in the world. Fibonacci trading devices analyze investors' behavior, so this index is one of the best products to analyze.

Turning Points and PHI-Ellipses

We start analyzing the S&P500 Index by using the PHI-ellipse as the standard geometric Fibonacci trading device. If this trading tool shows clear market patterns, we will integrate other trading tools with it.

As we explained earlier for the DAX30 Index, market pricing must stay within the PHI-ellipse from the beginning to the final point.

Figure 8.6 shows that there can be smaller PHI-ellipses within a bigger PHI-ellipse. The bigger the PHI-ellipse, the more powerful the trend reversals will be, once the market price reaches the end of that ellipse.

The WINPHI computer program is necessary to draw the PHI-ellipses.

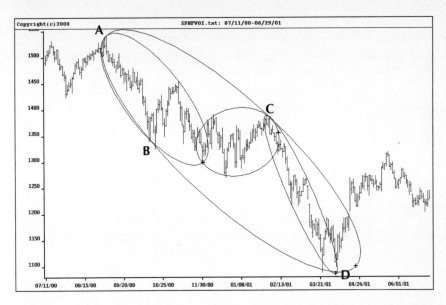

Figure 8.6   S&P500 Index from 07–00 to 06–01. *Source:* **FAM Research, 2000.**

Turning Points and Multiple Fibonacci Tools

In Figure 8.7, we show that the Fibonacci trading tools can be used for the S&P500 Index in exactly the same way that we used them for the DAX30 Index in the previous example.

After market price movements have been analyzed through the basic structure of the PHI-ellipse, we can look for multiple confirmations of the final point of the PHI-ellipse by integrating other Fibonacci trading tools.

We use a combination of a PHI-spiral, an extension, a PHI-channel, and a Fibonacci time-goal day. Those four geometric Fibonacci trading tools complement each other *and* the initial PHI-ellipse; thus, they provide additional evidence that trading according to Fibonacci rules and principles becomes safer and more reliable when more of the six possible Fibonacci trading tools confirm one and the same turning point in a market.

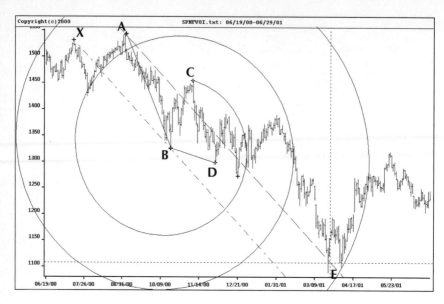

Figure 8.7   S&P500 Index from 06–00 to 06–01. *Source:* **FAM Research, 2000.**

1. PHI-spiral (see Chapter 6)
   The PHI-spiral has its center at point B and its starting point at C. The third PHI-spiral ring, turning clockwise, confirms the end of the PHI-ellipse at point E. (We do not show the second PHI-spiral, which creates the crossover point.)

2. Extension (see Chapter 3)
   The price goal with extension is calculated when we multiply the distance from point A to point B by the Fibonacci ratio 1.000. The price target is almost identical with the lowest low of the market at point E.

3. PHI-channel (see Chapter 4)
   The PHI-channel's baseline is from point X to point B and the outside point at peak A. The outside PHI-channel line also confirms the market bottom at point E.

4. Fibonacci time-goal day (see Chapter 7)
   When we multiply the distance from the valley at point B to the valley at point D by the Fibonacci ratio 2.618, we also identify the low of the market price at point E, using the Fibonacci time-goal day analysis.

Hourly Analysis of the S&P500 Index

The structures of the Fibonacci trading devices do not change, regardless of whether we work with weekly, daily, hourly, or 15-minute data. Here, we reiterate that traders should remember to consider daily data when they are basing trading decisions on hourly data.

Turning Points and PHI-Ellipses

Figure 8.8 shows the S&P500 Index during 18 weeks of hourly data.

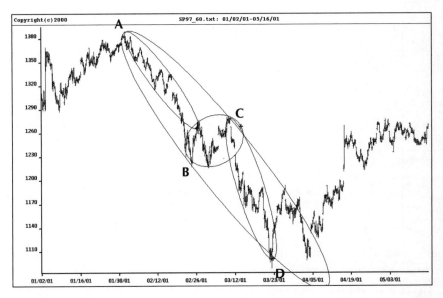

Figure 8.8 S&P500 Index from 01–01 to 05–01. *Source:* **FAM Research, 2000.**

The dramatic downturn in the S&P500 Index in February and March, 2001, is well captured by a set of PHI-ellipses.

In this chart, the hourly price patterns yield a much clearer analysis with the PHI-ellipse than with daily data. The final point at the valley at point D on the hourly chart is identical to the final point D as we analyzed it on the S&P500 Index chart using daily data (Figure 8.6).

Turning Points and Multiple Fibonacci Tools

Figure 8.9 demonstrates that Fibonacci trading devices can work independently of a particular data compression. Using hourly data, price and time goals are calculated in the same way as daily data.

To identify significant turning points in the S&P500 Index and receive multiple confirmations, PHI-ellipses can be supplemented by a combination of a PHI-spiral, an extension, a PHI-channel, and a time band of Fibonacci time-goal days.

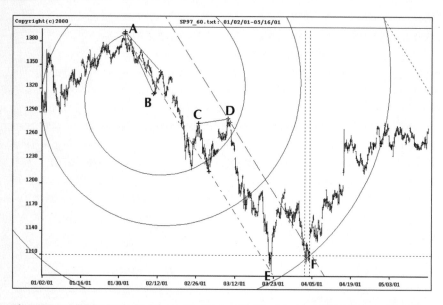

Figure 8.9 S&P500 Index from 01–01 to 05–01. *Source:* FAM Research, 2000.

1. PHI-spiral (see Chapter 6)
   The PHI-spiral has its center at point B and its starting point at point A. The third PHI-spiral ring, turning counterclockwise, confirms the end of the PHI-ellipse at the valley at point F. (We do not show the second PHI-spiral that creates the crossover point.)

2. Extension (see Chapter 3)
   The price goal with extension is calculated when we multiply the distance from point A to point B by the Fibonacci ratio 2.618. The price target pinpoints the market low at point F.

3. PHI-channel (see Chapter 4)
   The PHI-channel has the baseline from points A to E and the outside point at peak D. The outside PHI-channel line also confirms the market low at point F.

4. Fibonacci time-goal days (see Chapter 7)
   In the time-goal day analysis, we multiply the distance from point C to point D by the Fibonacci ratio 1.618. The market low at point F is also confirmed by this Fibonacci trading tool.

FINAL REMARKS

The quality of the Fibonacci analysis is independent of the data compression rate we choose. Geometric Fibonacci devices work equally well on weekly, daily, or intraday data, and independent of the type of product selected. Stocks, futures, and cash currencies can be traded, as long as the products are volatile and have enough liquidity to trade. Fibonacci trading tools do not work very well if there are no big price moves up or down.

We show that traders can invest either with the trend direction or in a countertrend. The trading tools are the same in both cases. Only the strategy changes.

Each Fibonacci analysis is started with a PHI-ellipse. When the other five geometric Fibonacci trading devices are combined with the initial PHI-ellipse analysis, they all fit together to form a profitable and reliable trading strategy.

It is important to know what to buy, but it is even more important to know when to buy. The same holds true on the sell side. This does not mean that there will be no losing trades. Every position entered should be protected with a stop-loss. However, Fibonacci trading tools are designed to keep the losses small and let the profits run. Fibonacci trading devices will always signal when to sell, either as a trailing stop or as a profit target. Very few trading tools provide this type of insight.

Working with Fibonacci trading tools is effective because they stay close to the market action. In contrast to technical analyses, Fibonacci trading tools are leading indicators. They show, in advance, what to do when special price levels are reached. The biggest challenge is simply to *believe* in them and to have the *patience* to wait for the correct signals.

Traders must always remember that although several trading tools might identify a potential trend change, the market may never reach the target price. Fibonacci trading tools point into the future, but it is still only a projected future. Trading opportunities may pass us by, but new opportunities for profitable investments will always continue to appear.

Before readers use our six geometric Fibonacci trading tools to invest, we highly recommend first working with the WINPHI software provided with the textbook. For registered members, we also have an online version of the WINPHI program at **www.fibotrader.com.** The Internet platform has the advantages of supplying a larger universe of trading vehicles from various liquid international markets in stocks, futures, and cash currencies, and allowing intraday analysis on 60-minute and 15-minute bases.

Fibonacci trading tools are all based on nature's law and human behavior. The actual market price never trades at the fair value of a product, and will either be too high or too low. Greed, fear, financial reports, government statistics, and the media are only some of the influences that move prices. Selling high and buying low at the right time is the secret. The six Fibonacci trading tools introduced in this workbook bring new Fibonacci traders closer to this secret.

Our geometrical Fibonacci trading tools work equally well on stocks, futures, stock index futures, or cash currencies, on weekly, daily, or intraday data, as long as there is volatility and liquidity. The Fibonacci trading tools, when correctly executed, give every investor the ability to make personal trading decisions independently of any other analysis available today, as long as he or she has the skill, patience, and discipline to work with these trading tools.

TUTORIAL

Readers who have reached these final pages might ask whether it was necessary to describe the Fibonacci trading tools in so much detail and with so many examples. The detailed explanations and numerous examples have been provided to demonstrate the strategy's reliability and consistency.

Traders who wish to work with the geometric Fibonacci trading tools online can go to our new Web site, which is available for registered members at **www.fibotrader.com.**

A feature of this Web site is a 15-minute slide-show/tutorial that includes:

1. Understanding the Fibonacci principle;

2. Crash course: Learning to use the WINPHI software;

3. How to work real-time with the trading tools: Two strategies;

4. Learning about the Web site: **www.fibotrader.com.**

We hope that the Web site will become a focal point for traders worldwide who are looking for successful trading tools, and who want to update their trading knowledge.